PENTECOST IF...

ANCIENT SECRETS AND TIMELESS TRUTHS TO RELEASE **PENTECOSTAL POWER** IN YOUR LIFE

ROD PARSLEY

DESTINY IMAGE® PUBLISHERS, INC.
P.O. Box 310, Shippensburg, PA 17257-0310
"Publishing cutting-edge prophetic resources to supernaturally empower the body of Christ"

This book and all other Destiny Image and Destiny Image Fiction books are available at Christian bookstores and distributors worldwide.

For more information on foreign distributors, call 717-532-3040.
Reach us on the Internet: www.destinyimage.com.

ISBN 13 TP: 978-0-7684-7301-8
ISBN 13 eBook: 978-0-7684-7849-5

For Worldwide Distribution, Printed in the U.S.A.
1 2 3 4 5 6 7 8 / 28 27 26 25 24

DEDICATION

With deep gratitude, I dedicate this volume to a lifelong friend, Ron Dailey. Ron's influence was instrumental at several pivotal points during my formative years of ministry. He encouraged me regarding television ministry, provided leadership for praise and worship, suggested that I conduct multiple services beginning in 1980, and introduced me to Dr. Norvel Hayes, which resulted in my sister Debbie's miraculous deliverance shared here in Chapter Four. I will forever be grateful for his indelible impact on my life.

CONTENTS

PREFACE

I am honored and thankful for the grace of God to allow me to release this volume as I celebrate my jubilee 50th year of gospel ministry. There are two quotes on the subject of Pentecost I have found useful over these past five decades that encapsulate my purpose in putting forth this work. The first is by A.W. Tozer: "The average Christian is so cold and so contented with his wretched conditions that there is no vacuum of desire into which the Holy Spirit can rush in satisfying fullness." The second is equally descriptive of what is possibly the greatest need in the modern church. The prince of preachers, Charles H. Spurgeon, made this emphatic statement: "Without the Spirit of God, we can do nothing; we are ships without wind or chariots without steeds; like branches without sap, we are withered."

Joel is regarded as the Old Testament prophet of Pentecost. This is his prophecy from chapter 2, verse 28 of the book that bears his name:

> *And it shall come to pass afterward, that I will pour out my spirit upon all flesh; and your sons and your daughters shall prophesy, your old men shall dream dreams, your young men shall see visions* (Joel 2:28 KJV).

It is in the New Testament book of Acts (or Action) where we as believers encounter a significant theological transition. In the gospels we have the record of God in Christ. When we leave the final verse of the gospel of John we enter Pentecostal headquarters where the God in Christ becomes the Christ in us. Here is a rather lengthy quotation, but I believe it is warranted as it includes important context. Here it is from Acts 2:1-18:

> *When the day of Pentecost had come, they were all together in one place. Suddenly a sound like a mighty rushing wind came from heaven, and it filled the whole house where they were sitting. There appeared to them tongues as of fire, being distributed and resting on each of them, and they were all filled with the Holy Spirit and began to speak in other tongues, as the Spirit enabled them to speak.*
>
> *Now dwelling in Jerusalem were Jews, devout men, from every nation under heaven. When this sound occurred, the crowd came together and were confounded, because each man heard them speaking in his own language. They were all amazed*

and marveled, saying to each other, "Are not all these who are speaking Galileans? How is it that we hear, each in our own native language? Parthians, Medes and Elamites, residents of Mesopotamia, Judea and Cappadocia, Pontus and Asia, Phrygia and Pamphylia, Egypt and the regions of Libya near Cyrene, and visitors from Rome, both Jews and proselytes, Cretans and Arabs—we hear them speaking in our own languages the mighty works of God." They were all amazed and perplexed, saying to each other, "What does this mean?"

Others mocking said, "These men are full of new wine."

But Peter, standing up with the eleven, lifted up his voice and said to them, "Men of Judea and all you who dwell in Jerusalem, let this be known to you, and listen to my words. For these are not drunk, as you suppose, since it is the third hour of the day. But this is what was spoken by the prophet Joel:

"'In the last days it shall be,' says God, 'that I will pour out My Spirit on all flesh; your sons and your daughters shall prophesy, your young men shall see visions, and your old men shall dream dreams. Even on My menservants and maidservants I will pour out My Spirit in those days; and they shall prophesy.'"

As I scan the spiritual landscape of America's churches I become acutely aware that it is parched wasteland where the command of Paul the apostle to be filled with the Spirit is either denied outright or largely ignored. It is an age when a powerless Pentecost has become the norm and not the exception. More perversion than power is on display on Sunday morning. More power brokers than prophets fill the pulpits, and more compromise than conviction is exhibited from those filling the pews. It is, therefore, incumbent upon us to plead for the living God, who condescends to indwell mortals, to come and fill us with His Holy Spirit. But perhaps we should first count the cost.

In the first century, Pentecost proved to be a dangerous proposition. Although it meant miraculous power available to the disciples of Christ, many times it also meant prison. Pentecost equipped them with enduement from heaven. It also carried with it orders of banishment from organized religion. The anointing of Pentecost was accompanied by the favor of God but often brought upon Jesus's followers the hatred of men. Pentecost produced the manifestation of miracles, signs, and wonders but it also created countless obstacles to be overcome.

Often I've wondered why it's necessary for us to erect a sign outside our churches to announce that we are Pentecostal. Could it be that absent such a sign we could not be identified? Is it that we need an indicator outside because there are no true signs ever witnessed inside? Is it that we, as congregants, are void of power, having been spoon-fed a steady diet of religious rhetoric? Are the clergy either afraid or ashamed to speak in tongues lest it offend a financially generous board member or cause a backslidden attender to become uncomfortable? Or perhaps the creative team has deemed the Holy

Spirit's presence to be, well, bad marketing? Allow me to be clear: the Holy Ghost does not need a new *definition*; He is in need of a new *demonstration*.

I have traveled to many American towns after they have been torn apart by a tornado. Let me assure you that I did not need anyone to inform me that a mighty wind had cleared the place. A fire is always self-announcing. Any believer who does not pray in the Spirit in private will display no supernatural power in public. Our spiritual impotence is due to our emptiness of heaven's language and causes us to be void of God's prophetic word.

Gone are pressed suits, exchanged for picnic clothes as we no longer pierce heaven and dethrone principalities and powers with our Pentecostal prayers of fire. We show off our shout and dance in the sanctuary yet possess no clout or demarcation in the Spirit. We claim authority but conquer no meaningful ground. We sing syrupy-sweet songs about our Christian experience more suitable for a junior high crush than true worship of our *Jehovah Izoz Hakaboth*, the Lord strong and mighty; *Jehovah Gador Milchamah*, the Lord mighty in battle; or *Jehovah Sabaoth*, God of the angel armies. What has our passionate Pentecostal praise devolved into? To our demise, we have become proficient in the dialect of a cursed culture but void of the voice of heaven.

There are those today who lay claim to the life-changing and earth-shattering, glorious and empowering baptism of the Holy Spirit. Yet they appear more dead than alive, more off than on, more wrong than right. Modern churchgoers seem to be more Spirit-frilled than Spirit-filled. They resemble a show pony more than a steed of war. It seems these have become more accustomed to the outer fringe of God's presence than possessing the inner essence of His holy fire and unequaled power.

It appears to me that whenever evil seeks to mire the work of God, our flesh always attempts to reassert itself, and our lack of fruit condemns our prayerless, powerless, passionless new version of Christ-less Christianity. Let us cry out at the altar of God for another outrageous, overpowering outpouring of Pentecostal power.

Before the day of Pentecost, Peter prayed for ten days and preached for ten minutes. Today we pray for ten minutes and preach for ten days. No wonder we have so many failures. It is now time for God's people to lose their dignity for a demonstration, their degrees for revelation, their reputation for repentance, their marketing for miracles, and their tongues of poison for tongues of fire. After all, the only reason to have a body is to express the life within it. That life is the indwelling of God's Holy Spirit. Pentecost if—øvvjonly if!

In Genesis 2:7, God *breathed* and man *became a living being*, and there was a brand-new beginning on earth. In Acts 2:2, God breathed again and gave us another new beginning on earth.

> *Suddenly a sound like a mighty rushing wind came from heaven, and it filled the whole house where they were sitting* (Acts 2:2).

As a 12-year-old boy, I sat cross-legged on the floor of our living room. My sister joined me; we were as close to the black and white television as my parents would allow as my dad carefully adjusted the rabbit-ear antenna for maximum picture clarity. Mom had popcorn and grape Kool-Aid ready. The aura of excitement and anticipation was palpable. Something truly historic was happening, and we were included!

It seemed like an eternity since July 16, 1969, when Apollo 11 launched from Cape Kennedy. A 38-year-old Ohio native, Neil Armstrong, was the commander. Joining him were the Command Module (Columbia) pilot Michael Collins and the Lunar Module (Eagle) pilot Buzz Aldrin. The world held its breath on July 20 as Eagle, with Neil Armstrong and Buzz Aldrin aboard, successfully landed on the lunar surface in the Sea of Tranquility. A quick breath and then we were spellbound again as Commander Neil Armstrong appeared descending the ladder. His first words are forever memorialized: "That's one small step for man, one giant leap for mankind." On July 24, 1969, Apollo 11 splashed into the Pacific Ocean with all three crew members. History had been made, and I was privileged to have witnessed it.

I have noticed distinct correlations between that historic launch and the day of Pentecost. First, there was a countdown. That of the Apollo mission distinctly echoes the heavenly anticipation of Pentecost. As the entire world waited with hearts pounding on July 16, 1969, so waited the disciples for the promised Holy Spirit. As the launch clock that day ticked down to zero, in like manner God's countdown from creation hit zero and the heavens were rent.

Second, there had to be an ignition, a spark, and the engines of the Apollo's rockets roared to life. On Pentecost there was no rocket fuel; but there was the fire of heaven.

Cloven tongues of fire sat on all of them, igniting their hearts with fervency, holiness, purity, and power.

Third, there was a rushing mighty wind. It swept the Apollo spacecraft upward, loosing her from the tethers that had bound the great craft to earth. So it was as the mighty rushing wind of the Holy Ghost loosed the 120 from the gravitational pull of religion and ritual, boardrooms and budgets. They were swept across every political, social, cultural, racial, denominational, and educational barrier as surely as Apollo 11 slipped the bondage of this blue marble planet. In fact, the destination of that space voyage mirrored Jesus coming to those first Pentecostals and to us. Apollo 11 was sent to earth's closest neighbor, the moon. The 120 were commissioned to go next door to everyone in Jerusalem, then further to Judea and Samaria, and then to the whole world.

Fourth, there came the blastoff! In July 1969, we watched for a few moments, and then they were out of sight. After the disciples blasted off, empowered by the Holy Ghost, they were everywhere! The fiery anointing of Pentecost had issued them a divine passport as ambassadors of the kingdom of Jehovah God and of His Christ. They were given total access and backstage passes. No one and no place was off-limits. They were possessors, not of the keys to the city but the keys of the kingdom. In the span of a few short years, without the aid of modernity, they had spread the gospel of Jesus Christ to the known world. Pentecost if—only if!

Now I put forth a daunting question: How might you respond if you entered a room filled with people and your presence went unnoticed and you were completely ignored?

Suppose this was no isolated situation and that it happened not once, but over and over again? To complicate the matter further, let's say you could easily overhear those present talking about you while refusing to interact with you. Then, when your presence was finally and grudgingly acknowledged, they referred to you as *it* instead of your appropriate pronoun, *he, she, him,* or *her.* What kind of effect would that have on you? No doubt you would look for those who, if they did not welcome you, at least recognized you.

This very scenario takes place in churches of all stripes every Sunday morning. It is the exact treatment regularly given to the Holy Spirit of God in Christian congregations and gatherings across the width and breadth of America and the world.

In a multitude of church services, congregants talk and sing about welcoming the Holy Spirit, desiring His presence, waiting for Him, and the like. However, when He graciously demonstrates Himself, those same individuals routinely disregard His presence and continue asking for Him to manifest. The wind of God is blowing east and they continue plowing ahead west under their own power, refusing to depart from their prearranged program, either click-tracked in their ear, written, or memorized. To capture the mighty rushing wind you must adjust your sails, lose your plan, and catch the breath of God. It is therefore not surprising that much of the church is living in spiritual decline and deficiency. In a word, stuck!

A fundamental difference between modern church culture and the kingdom of God is that in God's kingdom, there are conditions that must be met before His promises are fulfilled.

There are no participation trophies given for simply attending Sunday morning—or these days, just watching online.

English students know the principle of grammar referred to as a conditional clause. As you might guess, a conditional clause is often begun by a conditional word such as *if*. The word sets out a condition that must be set in motion in order for a future action, condition, or scenario to be fulfilled. Here is an example: "If it doesn't rain today, I will mow the yard this evening." A future action (mowing the yard) is dependent upon a condition (rain), which may (or may not) be fulfilled.

As was the case in my last book, *Revival If...,* I have chosen a conditional passage from the Bible for this work. It is found in Romans 8:11:

> But if the Spirit of Him who raised Jesus from the dead lives in you, He who raised Christ from the dead will also give life to your mortal bodies through His Spirit that lives in you.

There can be no doubt that the life-giving force behind the resurrection of Jesus Christ from the dead was the Holy Spirit. The Lord God is that Spirit (2 Corinthians 3:17). The Holy Spirit animated the earthly ministry of Jesus Christ from the moment He was baptized by John the Baptist (Luke 3:22) until He returned to heaven. This is the same Holy Spirit who moved at creation's dawn (Genesis 1:2). The same Holy Spirit lives in us today if—only if—we have genuinely placed our faith and trust in Jesus Christ as Savior and received the baptism of the Holy Spirit. If He lives within us, He will energize us with the life of God that He gave to the Lord Jesus. If we say we have His Spirit in us, yet we fail to demonstrate the life of Christ, something is decidedly amiss—and we agree, I am certain, the fault does not lie with our living, life-giving Creator, *Jehovah Bara*.

Nothing in the creation of God is without a divine plan and purpose. Sadly—however, I believe, reversibly—great numbers in the modern church have co-opted God's plan and purposes, selfishly twisting them to be all about them— their fulfillment and satisfaction, their blessing and self-will. Make no mistake, the living God certainly desires for all of us to have fulfillment, satisfaction, and blessing; yet the only way this becomes possible is for us to align with His divine will. We must cease attempting to use our sovereign God as a means to accomplish our own will and desires. This is the diabolical and deadly lie of secular humanism gone to seed— that we mere humans, without the Holy Spirit, can discern right from wrong. It is sheer idolatry to imagine that we have the strength and the wisdom to govern ourselves. This is a kingdom of God impossibility. In ancient Eden, the first man created, Adam, discovered this reality to his dismay in an incident recorded in Genesis 3.

The ultimate purpose of God's apex creation (human persons) is to contain the Creator (God). That purpose manifested is for each of us to display His character and nature on earth—indeed, in the place where He has commissioned us as ambassadors of His kingdom. This is possible and even probable as we yield to and depend upon Almighty God's indwelling presence by the Holy Spirit. It is an impossibility any other way—history is littered with the unsuccessful efforts of those who have attempted it in their own strength, intellect, or will.

We have great need of the baptism in the Holy Spirit. Pentecost if—only if! Our dependence must never be in the works of our flesh, regardless of what religious robes surround them. That Holy Spirit is God the Spirit who was in human form Jesus Christ. The baptism in the Holy Ghost is God through Jesus Christ returning to earth to live within us (John 14:16-17)—to tabernacle within our mortal body, to enable and empower us to live the Christ life in this world. We are the apex creation of Jehovah God, and the purpose of Pentecost is that the Holy Spirit within us may conform us into the image of Christ Jesus. To *conform* is "to behave according to the standards of God's kingdom." Holiness (power) is expressed by our conformity to our Savior's image. The only one who can convict our hearts of sin and of righteousness is the blessed Holy Spirit (John 16:8). No human standard—cultural, legal, or religious—will ever come close to meeting the requirements of our holy God. In addition, it is only the Holy Ghost who can cause us to see sin as God sees it—intolerable, unbearable, and deadly (Romans 6:23). To affirm that we can reach God's standard of holiness any other way is to renounce our dependence upon His Spirit and set ourselves up as our own Savior. What folly! And yet today, millions are treading this terminally lethal path. This is the apex of idolatry fully expressed.

God forbid that our generation should be as those whom Stephen accused, as he spoke in his own defense against false charges, recorded in Acts 7:51 (AMP): "You stiff-necked and stubborn people, uncircumcised in heart and ears, you are always actively resisting the Holy Spirit. You are doing just as your fathers did."

It is far past time for a paradigm shift regarding the Holy Spirit. I pray that we find ourselves among that willing throng who enthusiastically welcome the Holy Ghost of God and never actively resist Him. What joy to submit ourselves to His directive and rely upon His divine guidance as we cling to His mighty hand.

We are ready, we are waiting, we are longing after You. We are desperate, we are broken, we are nothing without You. Holy Spirit, come—come now, send the rain, bring the cloud. We want Your presence. Holy Spirit, come—come now, rend the skies, shake the ground, we want Your presence.

We are hungry, we are thirsty, we are yearning after You. We are desperate, we are broken, we are nothing without You. We bid You come like fire, we bid You come like rain, we bid You come in power, fill our hearts again. Holy Spirit, come—come now; bring the fire and shake the ground. We want Your presence.[1]

The above lyrics are a beautiful anthem of invitation for the Holy Spirit's presence to dwell among us. They were penned by my creative and anointed daughter, Ashton Parsley, along with Mark Arthur II, a lifelong member of World Harvest Church and integral member of Harvest Music Live.

Allow me to now point the pathway to the past, present, and future power of Pentecost if—only if!

FOREWORD

Pastor Rod Parsley, in a time when a generation stood in great need of a spiritual father to ignite young men and women to carry the mantle of Pentecost, succeeded in activating a global movement committed to spreading the gospel of Jesus with the power that descended on the day of Pentecost. I was one of the young people profoundly impacted by this great general of the faith.

As Christians, we are children of the cross, fruit of the empty tomb, and products of the upper room. The message of *Pentecost If…* affirms that the power of Pentecost is not confined to the pages of history but is a living reality for believers today. When we are filled with the Holy Spirit, we receive fresh oil, fire, and the breath of God—the Ruach, the Pneuma, the Paraclete. This empowerment transforms our lives in profound ways.

First, we live lives full of power, as evidenced by the early church's boldness and miraculous works after being filled with the Holy Spirit (Acts 1:8). This power is not merely for spiritual gifts but is foundational for our witness and daily walk with God. We also live in freedom, not bound by the chains of sin or oppression, as where the Spirit of the Lord is, there is liberty (2 Corinthians 3:17). This freedom allows us to break free from the past and live fully in the grace and truth of Jesus Christ.

Righteousness becomes our standard, as the Holy Spirit guides us into all truth and empowers us to live holy lives (Romans 14:17). This righteousness is not self-righteousness but a genuine transformation of character and conduct, reflecting the nature of Christ in our daily lives. Victory defines our existence, as we are more than conquerors through Him who loved us (Romans 8:37). This victory is not just over sin and death but extends to every area of life, giving us the confidence to face challenges with unwavering faith.

Finally, we live as anointed vessels, set apart and equipped for every good work (1 John 2:27). This anointing is not just for pastors or leaders but for every believer, empowering us to serve God and others with supernatural grace and effectiveness. The anointing teaches, guides, and remains with us, ensuring that we are never alone in our journey of faith.

More than ever, our world is in desperate need of a fresh outpouring of the Holy Spirit. In this crucial hour, it is vital to remember that the most powerful spirit on the planet is not that of Jezebel, Ahab, Baal, Goliath, Nebuchadnezzar, Herod, or even the Antichrist. The most powerful spirit on the planet is still the Holy Spirit of Almighty God.

It's time for a fresh Pentecostal outpouring. This book is beyond a must-read; it is a must-do, a must-execute. *Pentecost If…*calls us to action, to live out the fullness of what God has promised through the outpouring of His Spirit. May this book inspire you to embrace the power of Pentecost and transform the world around you. Through its pages, let us be reminded that with the Holy Spirit's empowerment, we can bring heaven to earth, advancing God's kingdom with boldness and compassion.

With a clarion call from this legendary spiritual father, let us do one thing together: in the name of Jesus and with the power of Pentecost, let's go change the world!

SAMUEL RODRIGUEZ
Lead Pastor of New Season
President/CEO of NHCLC
Author of *Your Mess, God's Miracle!*
Executive Producer of *Breakthrough*
and *Flamin' Hot* Movies

INTRODUCTION

The emotions of Christ Jesus's disciples had been shaken up and down and back and forth multiple times in the past few weeks. They had experienced His triumphant entry into the Holy City of Jerusalem as the thronging masses showered Him with adoring accolades. The Lord Jesus had informed them that they would rule and reign with Him in His kingdom, and in their understandably excited hearts they expected His words to be fulfilled any day now. Their unbounded disappointment flooded their entire beings when less than a week later, those same crowds who had exalted Him with their praise now shouted vicious and violent mockery at Him as they demonstrated, demanding His crucifixion.

The mob got their "justice." A weak-willed Roman governor caved in to their demonic demands, and without a shred of credible evidence, hearing their tumult and seeing their rage, Pilate sentenced Jesus of Nazareth to death. The living Christ of God was impaled upon an angry cross. He hung between heaven and earth between two common criminals in a grisly display of the despicable duplicity of the religious leaders mingled like poison with the might of imperial Rome.

Jesus's disciples were undone, abandoned, and lost without their Messiah to follow. They no longer sought seats of authority, but scurried away seeking safety in obscurity, in mortal fear of the Roman legions and the Sanhedrin's minions. When reports of His resurrection began to percolate through their group, and even though Jesus rehearsed it with them beforehand, their minds could not conceive, nor could their hearts dare to believe it. They hid themselves in secret places and hoped they would be able to escape unnoticed and unrecognized as the associates of a discredited and executed insurrectionist.

When He showed Himself alive to them, their gloomy defeat was turned to glorious delight. Surely His kingdom would now appear. They were sure of it! The resurrected King Jesus revealed Himself to them at intervals through the next 40 days of preparation. They were beside themselves with excited anticipation, and then He was gone again— transported through the atmosphere into heaven, with an angelic promise of His return in a similar fashion someday. He departed their company, but not before giving them a command and a caution.

The command was to *go* into all the world to preach the message of the gospel, which He had taught them in word and deed. The caution was to *not go* anywhere until Pentecost. They were still completely unprepared for their divine assignment. There was something else of absolute necessity He wanted them to have that they could not receive until then. He had explained to them the what and the why, but their minds were still reeling from the events of the past turbulent and traumatic six weeks. His instructions to them were still shrouded in uncertainty. The only thing they could do to bring clarity to the whole situation was to meticulously follow His instructions. So, they watched and waited. They didn't have to wait long. Just ten days later, on the second Sunday, morning broke and the sun rose on the day of Pentecost. Nothing would ever be the same.

How is it that a ragtag group of 11 men (12, with the addition of Matthias) would become a force so mighty that it changed the entire world and human history forever? What was it that affected such dramatic transformation that they were instantaneously changed from a weak, wary, and weary pack of fugitives into a band of brothers whose mission was to change the entire world by changing millions of lives, one at a time? Something radical and otherworldly had to happen to them for such a revolutionary alteration to take place. Within a single generation, the message of the gospel of Jesus Christ had spread like wildfire from a handful of followers in Jerusalem to every inch of the known world, including Mars Hill and the Roman Senate. What was the supernatural, mighty, unseen motive force behind it all?

The Lord's disciple Peter went from warming his shivering body by a fire and cowering in fear of being recognized by a little servant girl in Caiphas's courtyard, to boldly and fearlessly preaching a public sermon during a Jewish feast that resulted in over three thousand salvations. I assure you that his profound and persuasive power was not from drinking his favorite caffeinated beverage that morning. Nor was his appeal from listening to a self-help podcast by a well-known internet influencer the night before. He had made no resolution to try harder and do better. He was influenced, sure enough. What outside influence could have caused him to experience such a dramatic transformation in such a short period?

Certainly the resurrection of the Lord Jesus from the tomb had a remarkable and indelible impact on him, as well as all the other disciples. But Peter did no preaching between the day of the ascension and the day of Pentecost. What force unalterably changed who he had been all of his life and transported him to an altogether different plane of human experience? If we can discover what happened to Peter, maybe, just maybe that same power can forever change us, too. Are the events that transpired on the first Pentecost still possible today? Is that transformative power still available to the followers of King Jesus? If so, can we be used to change our world one life at a time here and now?

It is my firm conviction that it is, and my intention to show you that we can and we will—if only we are willing.

CHAPTER ONE

A PENTECOST PRIMER

Nothing they had previously seen or imagined could have ever prepared them for the drama that manifested upon Mount Sinai. The spectacle is revealed to us in the biblical narrative of Moses and the children of Israel in Exodus 19 and beyond. In the howling wilderness of Sinai, there was a mountain of fire. Smoke poured from every crevice, forming a billowing cloud that blocked their view of anything else. Bolts of lightning split the sky, and rolling thunder shook the earth as a rat terrier shakes a mouse. They attempted to compare it to any natural phenomenon that they had experienced before to no avail. No, nothing could compare to this divine display. Almighty God had personally descended to inhabit the summit of Mount Sinai, exactly as He had announced He would.

Suddenly, the weighty and piercing single note of a heavenly trumpet blasted forth from the towering heights, swelling with ever-increasing volume. At the apex, as the captivated eyewitnesses' ability to take in any more reached their limit, Moses broke his silence. He said that Jehovah had commanded him to ascend to the mount to meet directly with Him. The people were relieved that Moses would be their mediator. They were well aware that it was not possible for them to approach the presence of Jehovah, the Creator of heaven and earth, and live.

This encounter was as historic as it was dramatic. At this point, they were completely unaware that the "children of Israel" were about to become the "nation of Israel." The new nation would be governed by a set of supernatural laws delivered by the one true and living God. The images and reality of their 430 years of brutal slavery in Egypt was only 50 days behind them. Everything they had known for generations was about to change forever.

The first of Jehovah's instructions to Moses atop the vibrating Mount Sinai included the Decalogue, or Ten Commandments, as well as intricately detailed directions for constructing the Tabernacle. A multitude of other divine directives followed, including:

- The appointment, separation, and duties of the priesthood
- Specific instructions regarding offerings
- Principles that would govern their affairs, both civil and spiritual

- Organizational structure of their encampments

- The seasonal cycle of divine celebrations

This final item included seven celebrations, or in Hebrew *mo'edim*, in three installments. Beginning in the spring, there were Passover, Unleavened Bread, and Firstfruits. Fifty days following was the Feast of Weeks, or Shavout, as it is known in Hebrew. Then, in the fall, the three feast seasons came to a conclusion with Trumpets, the Day of Atonement, and Tabernacles—Rosh Hashana, Yom Kippur, and Sukkot, respectively.

We will focus here on the fourth of the seven celebrations, which is the Feast of Weeks. Its designation is derived as a result of its date being determined, according to Leviticus 23:15-16, by counting seven weeks plus one day from "the Sabbath," or Shabbat. There has been tremendous discussion and no less than three separate viewpoints of how this instruction should be determined. Scholars, as is often the case, have still not come to a consensus about it. For the sake of our discussion, let us conclude that the Feast of Weeks is 50 days after Firstfruits. (Firstfruits, of course, while also being one of the seven feasts, also became significant for another important reason—it was on that glorious day that the Lord Jesus Christ was resurrected from the dead.) The Feast of Weeks, or Shavout, was intended to be a celebration of the wheat harvest. A portion of the offering during this *mo'edim* was two loaves of bread, baked with leaven.

Of course, the agricultural aspect of this was in the future, since Israel was not in a position to plant or harvest anything in the middle of the mountainous wilderness. However, what they did receive on this day, according to rabbinic tradition, was the Law, divinely dictated to Moses by Jehovah Himself. It is this act of lawgiving by God, and its acceptance by the Jewish people, that has traditionally defined their beginning as a nation.

Once they had taken up residence in their land of promise, Israel was to continue to observe the Feast of Weeks in perpetuity as prescribed, bringing their offerings to celebrate God granting an abundant harvest. After the first Temple was destroyed and the Jews were exiled in Babylon, the emphasis returned to celebrating receiving the Law on that day.

There's an additional aspect of the Feast of Weeks, which we now know as the day of Pentecost, since the Greek term for *fiftieth day* is Pentecost. Here is an excerpt from my book *God's End-Time Calendar: The Prophetic Meaning Behind Celestial Events and Seasons*:

> There is another meaning to the great Feast of Pentecost...Remember, God Almighty commanded that the two loaves of bread that were to be waved before the Lord were to be made with leaven. God purposely left out the aspect of sin in this holy festival. But why? What was He saying to His people?
>
> You will recall that in the latter part of the harvest of Israel, God desired that His people remember the outsiders. By leaving the leaven in

the bread offering, He was reminding His people that the Gentiles—those "leavened" ones who were outside "unleavened" Israel—were going to be welcomed too...

Those two loaves represent sinful humanity. They represent men with the sinful nature "baked" into them. But God has mercy on all sinners! He has made a way for everyone to come to Him, through Jesus Christ.[2]

I find it fascinating that Jehovah God followed His instructions about the Feast of Weeks immediately with these additional instructions, from Leviticus 23:22:

> *When you reap the harvest of your land, you shall not reap your field up to the edge, nor shall you gather any gleaning of your harvest. You shall leave them to the poor and to the foreigner: I am the Lord your God.*

Here are a few final thoughts about this from *God's End-Time Calendar:*

> God is not only thinking of His chosen people here. His heart is turned toward everyone, the great unwashed majority of humanity, because He desires that not one should perish (2 Peter 3:9).

> Can you hear Him speaking to His people, instructing them, "Remember the Gentiles?" Remember that you are blessed to be a blessing. Remember that I intend to redeem the whole

earth, not just Israel. Don't forget them, rich and poor, in all that you do, even in how you bring in the harvests I give you.[3]

Indeed, our great God has always had the world that He created and His apex creation, the human race, in His heart and on His mind. This divine master plan for Shavout or Pentecost would find a full and final fulfillment in yet another supernaturally epic event that would take place many hundreds of years into the future. The Holy Spirit would make an indelible, fiery mark on this harvest celebration in another quite earth-changing and history-making demonstration of His creative capability. However, before we get there, I want to direct your attention to another consequential landmark on the road to Acts 2.

The Old Testament prophets of God were perpetually in a dilemma. There were instances when they commanded the attention and respect of kings, yet in many cases they were despised and disregarded and often considered deranged. Regardless of how men thought of them, they were the anointed and designated mouthpieces of Jehovah God, so much so that the Lord God repeatedly referred to them as "My servants the prophets."

Even in the New Testament, King Herod (not Herod the Great, but his son Herod Antipas) was by turns fascinated and horrified by one such prophet—namely, John the Baptist. Even though Herod eventually gave the order for John to be beheaded, Mark 6:20 says, "Herod feared John, knowing that he was a righteous and holy man, and protected him. When he heard him, he was greatly perplexed, but heard him gladly."

God often commissioned His true prophets to carry messages that were as unpopular as they were necessary. Having been given divine insight into future events, they would regularly prophesy about things well in advance of their manifestation. In some instances, they would deliver their divine messages at the same time as or even within another message that dealt with current events.

Such was the case with the minor prophet Joel, the son of Pethuel. He was assigned to minister to the southern kingdom of Judah during a time of tremendous national crisis—an invasion by the Babylonians. As Joel was describing the devastation and destruction the invaders would surely cause, he sounded an alarm for intercession. Then, as nearly every prophetic message does, he included an encouraging word of restoration and hope.

However, that is not all. In the middle of Joel's prophetic proclamation regarding the invasion of Judah and its aftermath, we read this stunning announcement in Joel 2:28-32:

> *And it will be that, afterwards, I will pour out My Spirit on all flesh; then your sons and your daughters will prophesy, your old men will dream dreams, and your young men will see visions. Even on the menservants and maidservants in those days I will pour out My Spirit. Then I will work wonders in the heavens and the earth—blood and fire and columns of smoke. The sun will be turned to darkness, and the moon to blood, before the great and awe-inspiring day of the Lord comes. And it will be that everyone who calls on the name of the Lord will be*

saved. For on Mount Zion and in Jerusalem there will be deliverance, as the Lord has said, and among the survivors whom the Lord calls.

Through the years, many have looked at this passage and relegated it to the large volume of prophetic utterances dealing with the events surrounding the end of human history. The apostle Peter, inspired by the same Holy Spirit who prompted Joel's powerful prophecy, had a different understanding of this passage. As we will examine shortly, there is a direct line from Joel 2 to Acts 2.

So, what transpired on the day of Pentecost as it's recorded in the Acts of the Apostles, chapter 2?

The earth-shaking day that the Lord Jesus apprised His disciples to expect had finally dawned. That diamond on a velvet couch, the Holy City of Jerusalem, was bustling and filled to overflowing for the yearly pilgrimage to the Feast of Pentecost. The atmosphere was electrified with pilgrims from all over the Mediterranean region. The focus was on the ceremonial waving of two loaves of leavened bread in the middle of the celebratory ceremony. But something extraordinary transpired that captured the startled attention of every attendant at the very beginning of the day's festivities.

It would prove to be a day of motion, emotion, and commotion! A rumbling like great claps of thunder from dark-throated storm clouds suddenly erupted, accompanied by the sound of a mighty rushing wind like a howling hurricane. People, most of them Galileans, began spilling out of a residential building speaking with loud voices in the various languages of the international guests. A stir arose among the throng about what was taking place, and how such a small group of individuals could be fluent in so many different languages. Some tried to explain the phenomenon by accusing the speakers of being intoxicated. However, it was unlikely that even the most intemperate would be overcome by drink at such an early hour in the day. Those among the masses were distinctly hearing different but fluent speech from the vast corners of the Roman world. Without exception, those speaking were extolling and magnifying the manifold virtues of the living, glorious, and almighty Jehovah God. It is no surprise that the thronging crowd continued to expand exponentially. It was verifiably and literally heaven touching earth.

The confusion had reached a fevered pitch and had nearly careened out of control when a man, surrounded by a handful of others, stepped forward and began to speak to the massive assembly. Said he:

> *Men of Judea and all you who dwell in Jerusalem, let this be known to you, and listen to my words. For these are not drunk, as you suppose, since it is the third hour of the day. But this is what was spoken by the prophet Joel* (Acts 2:14-16).

The apostle Peter continued declaring boldly and forcefully what Joel prophesied many hundreds of years prior. It was this very day in this very place on this blue marble planet coming to pass before their witnessing eyes and listening ears. The Holy Spirit prophesied by Joel, promised by God, and proclaimed by Jesus Christ was in this moment being poured out upon them and their children after them. Astounding, supernatural events began to occur, and signs, wonders, and miracles began to take place routinely and with astounding regularity. Ordinary people were having extraordinary insight into the plans and purposes of God. It seemed that no one was left out or left behind. In addition to all this, the culmination of this great outpouring would explode into a revival of presence, praise, and power such as this world and its human family had never been partakers.

The former cowardly Peter, now transformed by the flaming fire of Pentecost, continued to preach a masterful message under a new and profound anointing. He proved to all those assembled that Jesus of Nazareth, who had been crucified just outside the city gates only a few weeks earlier, was indeed and without question the Christ who was prophesied throughout the Holy Scriptures. Peter's words were fearless and forceful, controversial and compelling, but most importantly, they were truth. They penetrated the hard and calloused hearts of their hearers, who were stricken immediately with Holy Ghost-inspired conviction and cried out for resolution in deep repentance. The former fisherman's answer was sufficiently succinct and dauntingly direct:

> Repent and be baptized, every one of you, in the name of Jesus Christ for the forgiveness of sins, and you shall receive the gift of the Holy Spirit. For the promise is to you, and to your children, and to all who are far away, as many as the Lord our God will call (Acts 2:38-39).

In the first evangelistic crusade, Peter's sermon lasted about ten minutes, but they had prayed for ten days. In the modern dry and dusty powerless faux church, we pray for ten minutes and preach for ten days. No wonder we have so many failures! As a result, three thousand were saved and came into the kingdom of God and of His Christ. King Jesus had returned to earth in the person of the Holy Ghost. There was presence and power, glory and gifts, manifestations and miracles. Everything had changed forever!

I can only imagine the answers they gave when their families at home asked them for descriptions of their trip to Jerusalem. They had made the yearly pilgrimage to the city bringing baskets full of Pentecost offerings, but they returned having encountered no gentle breeze of spring but a hurricane from heaven. It was the same uncontrollable wind that had split the Red Sea and afforded them a highway of dry land but swallowed Pharaoh's army. They went back home transformed by tongues of fire that had rested upon each one. It was no faint flicker but a blazing inferno of consecration. They now wore the brand of the Holy Ghost of God. They now spoke the languages of the nations and of the Spirit. The gospel was about to go global!

Once again, I will include a brief excerpt from *God's End-Time Calendar*:

> Can you think of a greater fulfillment of God's passion for the lost Gentile world than for a new covenant church comprised of every tribe and tongue? Oh, how beautifully and perfectly the Day of Pentecost fulfills the heart of God expressed in the Feast of Weeks. What better fulfillment of the twin symbols of harvest and leavened bread, than a harvest of Gentiles, filled

with the Spirit of the living God, added to the Israelites, the chosen people of God? This is truly the glorious church as God intends it.[4]

The account of the day of Pentecost given to us in Acts 2 had two preeminent outcomes—the first of which was immediate. As we have seen, many thousands of the multitude who had assembled from sheer curiosity to witness the supernatural in Jerusalem that day were convicted of their sin, repented, and were gloriously born again. This was the initial result of the indwelling and empowering of the Holy Ghost, exactly as Jesus related it to His disciples just before His ascension back to heaven. A divine "go" had flooded their waiting hearts, minds, and feet because of Christ's passion to reach the world. That same passion now inundated their beings by the presence of the Holy Ghost taking up residence within their mortal bodies, quickening them and making them alive.

Those who initially received the baptism of the Holy Spirit were issued supernatural offensive and defensive equipment to accomplish every task for which they had been commissioned by heaven. They had received a new passport delivered by the kingdom of God. They were installed as ambassadors with all the appropriate rights and privileges. Their security was provided by Jehovah Sabaoth, the God of the angel armies. There were no academic, racial, cultural, religious, or language barriers left standing when that mighty wind blew. Storms could not stop them, prisons could not hold them, snakes could not kill them, and demons could not hinder them. They were on the move. Nothing was stagnant, slow, or stalled. They were out in the open and unhindered by anything or anyone. They were everywhere, and Jesus Christ, who was with them, was now in them to do and will of His own good pleasure (Philippians 2:13). He was working with them, confirming His Word with signs following (Mark 16:20). Whether they went to their own families or to other nations, their testimony was confirmed by remarkable demonstrations of divine power. That power gave credibility to the words they spoke, which could not be dismissed nor reasoned away.

Within a single generation, the gospel of the living Christ had spread from its origin with 120 in the upper room in Jerusalem to the expanse and entirety of the known world. Its appeal was in no way segregated to any particular ethnic group, region, or demographic, but to everyone, from every culture and every country where these fire baptized Christ-ones were sent.

Acts 13:1 briefly references a believer named Manaen, who was a leader at the church in Antioch who had been brought up with Herod the tetrarch. (We know that the gospel of Christ was not unknown in Herod's household, since Luke 8:3 identifies Joanna, the wife of Herod's steward, supporting the ministry of the Lord Jesus.)

The apostle Paul preached the gospel on Mars Hill in Athens, where the most learned and intellectual men of the day gathered for discourse and debate. Paul unashamedly told them that he perceived they were too religious (superstitious) (Acts 17:22). Paul also testified of his faith in Jesus Christ before kings like Agrippa and Festus (Acts 26). Eventually he defended his faith in Rome (Acts 28), where he presumably presented his case to the emperor.

The final portion of Acts chapter 8, verses 26-40, records for us how the treasurer of the nation of Ethiopia was converted and baptized. This official had an encounter with Philip, who had been given a word of direction by the Holy Ghost to travel from Jerusalem to Gaza. Philip was an evangelist who led the entire city of Samaria in revival without the aid of television, social media, or radio. He had no staff, building, finance committee, mailing list, platform, or public address system. What he did have was the mighty baptism of Pentecost and a divine go! Who can tell what widespread impact the newly converted Ethiopian, a person of stature and influence, must have had in that entire nation for the gospel of Christ?

Let us remember also the multitudes of men and women who were convicted of their sin and who repented, were forgiven, and ushered into the kingdom of God in that first monumental outpouring of the Holy Ghost in Acts 2. They were Jews and proselytes (new converts to Judaism) from every nation (Acts 2:10), and they returned home with an on-fire, up-to-date testimony of their faith in Jesus Christ, which they no doubt shared with their friends, family, and everyone they encountered.

This kind of supernatural, heaven-sent, and Holy Ghost-delivered growth was not only unprecedented, it was unforeseen by everyone except King Jesus. He could not have been more clear with His disciples regarding the "go" that would enter their lives. He knew it would also cause them to become witnesses to their faith first in Jerusalem, then in Judea, Samaria, and then to the uttermost parts of the earth (Acts 1:8). By every measurable standard, the church of the living Christ through the power of the Holy Ghost given at Pentecost had fulfilled that requirement before one generation had passed. Despite torrents of formidable opposition from the kingdom of satan and widespread persecution, the church of Pentecost prevailed and prospered by the empowering of the Holy Ghost of God.

> *I was standing on the banks of the river,*
> *Looking out over life's troubled sea,*
> *When I saw an old ship that was sailing,*
> *Is that the old ship of Zion I see?*
> *Its hull was bent and battered,*
> *From the storms of life, I could see;*
> *Waves were rough, But that*
> *old ship was sailing,*
> *Is that the old ship of Zion I see?*
> *At the stern of the ship was the captain,*
> *I could hear as he called out my name;*
> *Get on board, it's the old ship of Zion,*
> *It will never pass this way again.*
> *As I step on board I'll be leaving,*
> *All my troubles and trials behind;*
> *I'll be safe with Jesus, the captain,*
> *Sailing out on the old ship of Zion.*[5]

Christ Jesus declared and decreed in Acts 1:8: "But you shall receive power when the Holy Spirit comes upon you. And you shall be My witnesses...."

Two words are of particular importance from this passage. In my opinion, they deserve additional explanation and distillation. They are totally fundamental to our understanding of how those who were tasked with the fulfillment of the Great Commission in those initial embryonic and inaugural years achieved such success.

The first of these is the word which is translated "power." Certainly you would agree that there exist many kinds or forms of power. But there is a particular and exceptional kind of power that the Lord Jesus told His followers they would receive as a result of what we now know as the baptism of the Holy Spirit. The Greek word *power* here is *dunamis*, meaning force, might, or ability. The same word is often used in the New Testament to describe the motive force behind miracles or other supernatural events. (The English words *dynamo, dynamic*, and *dynamite* each derive their origin from the Greek word *dunamis*.) The same word is also used in Ephesians 1:19-20 to describe Jesus Christ being raised from the dead:

> *And what is the surpassing greatness of His power toward us who believe, according to the working of His mighty power, which He performed in Christ when He raised Him from the dead and seated Him at His own right hand in the heavenly places.*

The power of God was sufficient to resurrect the three-days-dead body of the Prince of God while satan himself and all the forces of hell conspired to keep Him in that cold, dark, sealed tomb. Surely that same power will overcome any other competing force arrayed against it. That is the superior power

Jesus of Nazareth promised to His disciples. That supernatural power would entitle them to go and permit them to do everything that He would direct and delegate them to do in the earth. Whatever you need to do or are called of God to accomplish may seem impossible. Remember that after Calvary, the resurrection of Jesus of Nazareth seemed even more impossible—so receive this powerful word now and be encouraged.

The church of Jesus Christ, including you, has been empowered by the Holy Spirit to go and to do whatever King Jesus directs us to do. The miracle-working power of *Jehovah Izoz Hakaboth*, the Lord strong and mighty, is what empowers us. It is not our intellect, our natural ability, our goodness, wealth, skill, expertise, courage, or any other natural advantage or attribute. The power of God is what makes you capable of fulfilling the will of God. Only that selfsame power that raised up Jesus Christ from the dead will enable us to fulfill God's will in our lives and in this world!

The second word I would like to draw your attention to is the word *witnesses*. Again, I am referencing the Greek word used here, which is *martus*, meaning "martyr or witness." The first image that comes to mind when one hears the term *martyr* is someone who gives their life for what they believe. In fact, many thousands over the centuries have laid down their lives for their faith in Jesus Christ—and unfortunately this trend, although rarely discussed, is accelerating in our world today.

Let's take a look at the term *witness*. Most often the first question that occurs to folks when hearing "witness" is, "What is the purpose of a witness?" Usually, the example from a court of law comes to mind. In fact, the seat next to the judge is aptly named the witness stand. When a witness is called to the stand in a court proceeding, they are required to testify. However, they are not permitted to talk about anything they want—they swear on oath or affirmation to tell only what they have seen and heard. They must not speculate. They cannot discuss what someone else has seen or heard. In other words, they produce evidence. (Evidence and proof are not exactly the same thing from a legal standpoint, but evidence can become proof.)

Think for a moment about a legal drama you may have seen. The judge presides over the courtroom. The witness is on the witness stand. The attorney asks the witness a series of questions demonstrating their relevance to the proceeding or the legal matter in question. For instance, let's say the witness was present when the accident that is being litigated occurred. The attorney leans in and asks, "Can you describe what happened when you approached the intersection?" The witness then describes what they have seen, heard, or experienced. Others may have a different point of view about what happened. They may doubt the credibility, honesty, or reliability of the witness. They may object to the remembrance of events the witness shared. None of these things can keep the witness from telling what they have seen and heard. That is the purpose of a witness in a courtroom. It is also the purpose of a Christian witness.

Jesus said you would receive power—miracle-working power. He went on to say that the purpose of that power was to be a witness—to tell what you have seen, heard, and experienced. If circumstances seem to align against you to keep you silent or tempt you to change your testimony, remember that the same power that raised Christ from the dead lives within you. The Holy Spirit of God is there to empower you or enable you to become vocal about what you know about Jesus of Nazareth. After all, He was resurrected from the dead and found you, forgave you, welcomed you and loves you, and gave you eternal life and heaven as your eternal home. Here's the riveting and revealing question: has God done anything for you? Tell someone your story—that's your witness, and it is the most powerful tool in proclaiming the Lordship of Jesus Christ.

Here is a biblical example. In John 9, the Lord Jesus healed a man who had been blind from birth. The religious leaders, as usual, became enraged because Jesus healed the man on the Sabbath. They claimed that according to the law of Moses that constituted work, so they concluded that Jesus was violating the commandment to keep the Sabbath holy. (Of course, this was only the letter of the law and not the intention, or spirit, of the law as it was designed by God.) The self-righteous leaders then turned their wrath toward the man whose eyes had been opened for the first time in his life. They railed upon Jesus, accusing Him of being a sinner Himself.

Here's the man's drop-the-mic answer, from John 9:25: "He said, 'I do not know if He [Jesus] is a sinner. I know one thing: I was blind, but now I see.'" This confounded and further enraged the religious leaders. The healed man's witness was simply telling his story. He was an effective witness because he testified to what he had personally experienced—what Jesus Christ had done for him. He didn't need to expound on the origins of the universe or how many angels could dance on the head of a bottle cap. He didn't have a PhD in Biblical Literature, but he knew he was blind and now he could see! Nobody with a shred of intellectual honesty or common sense could say that he was not a powerful witness and that he not was telling the truth.

Here is another example, perhaps a bit better known—it's from Acts 3. Peter and John encountered a lame man at the Temple gate. The man was miraculously healed by the power of God. Enter once again the religious leaders. They summarily arrested all three of them and forthwith locked them in jail. The next day the apostles were examined about the incident, and they testified that it was the power of the resurrected Christ that caused the lame man to be healed. The self-righteous critics were baffled and quite uncertain how to respond. Acts 4:13-14 says:

> *When they saw the boldness of Peter and John and perceived that they were illiterate and uneducated men, they marveled. And they recognized that they had been with Jesus. But seeing the man who was healed standing with them, they had nothing to say against it.*

The man who had been healed gave a simple but stunning witness of his own story, which he accomplished by just standing up. He had been lame from birth and had never stood on his own feet or walked in his entire life, and he was over 40 years old. We don't know how long he had been begging at the Temple gate, but it was surely long enough that everyone who used that gate recognized him. Now he was walking just as well as anyone else. His testimony was so shockingly real and the truth of the Holy Spirit's power was so evident that five thousand men, and an unknown number of women and children, were immediately swept into the kingdom of God as a result!

Think of all the supernatural things that King Jesus has done in your life. Who knows what glorious miracles will happen as a result of your witness—by all of us in great honesty, empowered by the Holy Ghost, just telling our story? It may not be as dramatic as the examples I mentioned, but it will be life-changing and eternity-altering for someone who hears how Jesus Christ changed your life. You are a witness, and your witness is supernaturally powerful—believe it!

CHAPTER TWO

PENTECOST THROUGH THE AGES

Anyone attempting to reconstruct events from thousands of years ago is at a disadvantage. Over the centuries, sources that may have been used in ages past have become lost for a multitude of reasons. The limited eyewitness sources that still exist gain additional credibility simply because they are among the only remaining testimonies of what happened during the time period being discussed. When relatively few reliable sources are the only ones available, differing points of view, or corroboration of those that survive, may be impossible to reconstruct with any degree of reliability.

So it is when trying to track down those who believed and received the baptism of the Holy Spirit from the close of the Acts narrative until the 20th century. In many cases, ancient writers made no mention of the baptism of the Holy Spirit at all. We must, therefore, rely on observances of miracles or the gifts of the Holy Spirit to determine whether or not believers in past ages continued to preach, teach, believe in, and receive the baptism of the Holy Ghost.

Justin Martyr, commenting in his *Dialogue with Trypho*, contended that prophecy was still active among the churches in his day.

> For the prophetical gifts remain with us, even to the present time. And hence you ought to understand that [the gifts] formerly among your nation have been transferred to us. And just as there were false prophets contemporaneous with your holy prophets, so are there now many false teachers amongst us, of whom our Lord forewarned us to beware.[6]

Irenaeus had this testimony regarding miracles in his day:

> Those who are in truth His disciples, receiving grace from Him, do in His name perform [miracles], so as to promote the welfare of other men, according to the gift which each one has received from Him. For some do certainly and truly drive out devils, so that those who have thus been cleansed from evil spirits frequently both believe [in Christ], and join themselves to the Church. Others have foreknowledge of things to come: they see visions, and utter prophetic expressions. Others still, heal the sick by

laying their hands upon them, and they are made whole. Yea, moreover, as I have said, the dead even have been raised up, and remained among us for many years…. The name of our Lord Jesus Christ even now confers benefits [upon men], and cures thoroughly and effectively all who anywhere believe on Him.[7]

Origen, a prolific writer and apologist for the Christian faith, declared that he had seen instances of healing, prophecy, and exorcism.

Chrysostom, a revered church father and skilled preacher, seemed to be lamenting the lack of speaking in tongues when he said in his commentary on Paul's epistles to the Corinthians:

> This whole place is very obscure; but the obscurity is produced by our ignorance of the facts referred to and by their cessation, being such as then used to occur but now no longer take place. And why do they not happen now? Why look now, the cause too of the obscurity hath produced us again another question: namely, why did they then happen, and now do so no more?[8]

Augustine commented that miracles still occurred in his lifetime, and that he was eyewitness to several of them. He mentions that they may not have the same effect as miracles recorded in the Bible, since there was no authority that could give them the same credibility.

One thing I should mention here is the Christian theological debate involving two opposing doctrines, namely cessationism and continuationism. The first believe that the gifts and ministries of the Holy Spirit have ceased. The second believe that these supernatural things of God have continued. Cessationists assert that miracles are far out of the ordinary and should not be expected by believers today, since God rarely chooses to intervene by such means any longer. They maintain that the gifts of the Holy Spirit, along with manifestations of miracles, were only necessary until the end of the apostolic age, and until the canon of Scripture was completed. Their argument is that once believers had a complete New Testament, miracles were no longer needed as confirmation that the living God was still at work in the earth. In addition, the ability to perform miracles was only enabled by the direct involvement of acknowledged apostles of the Lord, and when those who had been set apart by those apostles died, miracles largely ceased to be operative among believers.

Without getting too far into the specifics here, the entire doctrine of cessationism began, as far as historians can tell, with John Calvin during the Protestant Reformation as a response to the claims of miracles taking place in the Roman Catholic Church. There can be no doubt, unfortunately, that at times churches, both in the ancient and contemporary worlds, have used reports of miracles, healings, and other supernatural interventions to generate interest and financial donations. Calvin apparently hoped to refute such errant sensationalism, which contributed to his development of the idea that the gifts of the Holy Spirit were no longer in operation and miracles on earth had concluded.

Another concern of cessationism is that revelatory gifts, such as prophecy, by definition ("a message from God") would require all such utterances to be given equal consideration with the canon of Scripture. Since the canon of Scripture is closed, prophecy must have ceased—otherwise, the Bible would still be subject to additions based on prophecy still being operative.

What cessationism fails to account for in this instance is that the Bible very clearly states the purpose of prophecy, according to 1 Corinthians 14:3: "But he who prophesies speaks to men for their edification and exhortation and comfort." Therefore, the purpose of prophecy is not to add to the Bible, but to encourage believers and confirm what the Bible teaches. Any prophetic utterance that does not adhere to the truths already revealed in scripture deserves no consideration. All prophecy must be judged by those who hear it to determine its legitimacy (1 Corinthians 14:29). Other translations say hearers should weigh, evaluate, discern, or pass judgment on what was said. Paul encourages all believers to desire to prophesy, according to 1 Corinthians 14:1 and 14:39. Why would he tell us to desire something if it is no longer available to us?

Cessationism also holds that the gifts of the Holy Spirit ceased because in the plan of God they were no longer necessary. On the other hand, I maintain that the gifts became rare because the church departed from apostolic doctrine and began to introduce aspects of pagan rituals and syncretism into its practices and programs. True doctrine was discouraged and dismissed, disregarded, or ignored, while other practices became widespread. Eventually a backlash against the corruption and corpulence of a bloated religious system gave rise to the Protestant Reformation. This set the stage for subsequent groups, such as Moravians, Methodists, and others, to be open to the involvement and influence of the Holy Spirit. These developments in turn led to the explosion of interest in the Holy Spirit, which had its beginning at the turn of the 20th century.

The Holy Spirit of God has certainly never gone away, nor has He ever been idle or disinterested. Remember, the Lord Jesus Himself said in John 14:16-17:

> *I will pray the Father, and He will give you another Counselor, that He may be with you forever: the Spirit of truth, whom the world cannot receive, for it does not see Him, neither does it know Him. But you know Him, for He lives with you and will be in you.*

Why is it, then, that His influence was rarely mentioned through entire ages of human history? We know that God intends for people of every age to receive the promise of the Holy Spirit. Peter, preaching on the day of Pentecost, said, as recorded in Acts 2:39: "For the promise is to you and to your children, and to all who are far away, as many as the Lord our God will call."

We discover a telling clue in Judges 2:7: "So the people served the Lord all the days of Joshua, and all the days of the elders who outlived Joshua, who had seen all the great works that the Lord had done for Israel." Verse 10 continues: "That entire generation passed away, and after them grew up a generation who did not know the Lord or the deeds that He had done for Israel."

The first generation to receive truth tends to hold it as a *conviction*. They will not compromise any truth that has resulted in their freedom. They will not tolerate anything that they perceive as a threat to the liberties they have been granted.

The second generation tends to view the same truth as only a *persuasion* rather than a conviction. In order for truth to be maintained, it must appeal to their rational mind and human reasoning. They, therefore, could be persuaded that something other than the truth is true.

By the third generation, the rapid decline continues and goes a step further, viewing truth as nothing more than an *opinion*. Since everyone has an opinion, and many have differing opinions regarding what is the truth, all opinions tend to be treated with the same deference. Eventually, regardless of how contrary, out of the ordinary, or bizarre an opinion may be, it will be afforded the same respect as any other opinion, giving room for, "your truth is not necessarily my truth," or a point where everyone possesses their own truth. By this time, truth is given no more regard than any assortment of mistruths, half-truths, and outright lies.

I believe this accurately describes at least one major reason that the emphasis on the Holy Spirit that we read about in the book of Acts and the Epistles was disregarded and discarded by immediate subsequent generations.

This regrettably disastrous sequence of decline is taking place again now in many various forms and locations. Individual believers and the church as a whole have become inwardly focused rather than outwardly focused. The emphasis is on self-serving in place of self-sacrificing. *Me* has become more important than *others*—and ultimately, more important than the presence and voice of *the Holy Ghost*.

The Holy Spirit will not strive: "And the Lord said, My spirit shall not always strive with man" (Genesis 6:3 KJV). He can be grieved and will not remain where He is not welcome: "And do not grieve the Holy Spirit of God, with whom you were sealed for the day of redemption" (Ephesians 4:30 NIV). The truth of the gospel of Christ is a great treasure, but one that must be given away rather than hoarded. It does not diminish with the giving—on the contrary, it increases.

While He walked among us, the Lord Jesus Christ gave us some significant insights into the person and purpose of the Holy Spirit. He gave us tremendous instruction about the Holy Spirit in the gospel of John.

> *I will pray the Father, and He will give you another Counselor, that He may be with you forever: the Spirit of truth, whom the world cannot receive, for it does not see Him, neither does it know Him. But you know Him, for He lives with you, and will be in you* (John 14:16-17).

> *I have spoken these things to you while I am still with you. But the Counselor, the Holy Spirit, whom the Father will send in My name, will teach you*

everything and remind you of all that I told you (John 14:25-26).

But when the Counselor comes, whom I shall send to you from the Father, the Spirit of truth who proceeds from the Father, He will bear witness of Me (John 15:26).

Nevertheless I tell you the truth: It is expedient for you that I go away. For if I do not go away, the Counselor will not come to you. But if I go, I will send Him to you. When He comes, He will convict the world of sin and of righteousness and of judgment: of sin, because they do not believe in Me; of righteousness, because I am going to My Father, and you will see Me no more; and of judgment, because the ruler of this world stands condemned.

I have yet many things to tell you, but you cannot bear them now. But when the Spirit of truth comes, He will guide you into all truth. For He will not speak on His own authority. But He will speak whatever He hears, and He will tell you things that are to come. He will glorify Me, for He will receive from Me and will declare it to you. All that the Father has is Mine. Therefore I said that He will take what is Mine and will declare it to you (John 16:7-15).

One of the most significant developments in the church at large during the 20th century, and continuing to the present day, is an exponential increase of revelation and understanding concerning our complete dependence upon the operation and activity of the Holy Spirit. And why not? King Jesus indicated that the Holy Ghost would be the active administrative agent of the Godhead on the earth during these last days. As such, I am not sure it would be possible to overemphasize His necessity, importance, and influence. I could go so far as to say that this is the age of the Holy Spirit. He is the Counselor of whom Jesus spoke. He is not, as I have often said, a third cousin twice removed, watered-down version of the Godhead. The Holy Spirit is God. He is not a thing, and certainly not one to be relegated to an inferior position or status. In fact, I have noticed this about many of the local churches that are most effective in fulfilling the Great Commission (Mark 16:15-18) and the Great Command (Matthew 22:37). They believe that their mission to reach their respective communities with the gospel of Jesus Christ is maintained by the utmost regard for the Holy Spirit. These churches bless Him and are utterly depending upon His power of convicting sin and convincing of righteousness.

Some of the hallmarks of these churches that I have recognized are:

- Unpredictable
- Exciting
- Abounding in signs, wonders, and miracles
- Effective
- Special targets of vitriol and hate

As for unpredictability, Jesus said to a Pharisee and ruler of the Jews called Nicodemus in John 3:8: "The wind blows where it wishes, and you hear its sound, but you do not know where it comes from or where it goes. So it is with everyone who is born of the Spirit." The Holy Spirit may blow in and rearrange everything in your life. Our posture as believers is not to ask God why He does something. It is to exhibit our obedient willingness to adjust our sails, catch the wind, and allow Him take us in the direction of His sovereign will.

Please understand that this element of unpredictability is never intended to sway our commitment to preparation and planning. Modern preachers have become infamous for blaming their ineffectiveness in the pulpit on the leading of the Holy Spirit. They may claim that the Holy Spirit's intervention required them to change direction at the last minute, resulting in a public display of the inadequacy of their preparedness. Truth be told, it was more likely their own lack of seriousness in seeking the face of God through the Holy Spirit and prayer. We should be serious in preparing for the most important interaction of the week—the weekly worship service. However, we must ever be alert to the leading of the Holy Spirit.

Oh, the multitude of occasions when I have sensed His divine presence and discerned His leading for me to set aside a fully prepared message to obey whatever He bids me to do. In that moment, our commitment to the high calling upon our lives demands that every gospel preacher be prepared. However, simultaneously they must be utterly dependent upon the anointing of the Holy Ghost should His supernatural agenda change. There is no greater joy than knowing that you have operated in lockstep with the plan crafted by the Creator of heaven and earth, have yielded to the Holy Ghost, and have declared His voice in the earth. Thereby, we experience firsthand the fulfillment of Philippians 2:13 (KJV), "For it is God which worketh in you both to will and to do of his good pleasure."

The unpredictability factor should find its expression in every aspect of our services. We should expect it from praying to worshiping in our singing and giving. We should experience it from preaching and teaching through the altar service. We should find it all accompanied by the gifts and fruit of the Holy Spirit on full display. Perhaps the blessed Holy Spirit releases His convicting power and the anointing to win souls at the beginning of the worship service rather than at the end? Shall we not follow His leading in joyous abandon? Suppose the worship music needs to be adjusted. We might not only allow but plead that the gifts of the Holy Ghost may be in dynamic manifestation and glorious demonstration at any point in our assemblies. Here's the question: does the modern church have time in its deplorable prescheduled minimal time allotment for the Holy Ghost to move? Will we make time for the wind, the sound, and the fire? Do we actually believe that the Holy Ghost is God, and is vibrantly and vitally alive and personally present? If we do, we can but acknowledge His sovereignty and give Him place and space to will and do of His own good pleasure.

Of course, there are sensible, spiritual, and scriptural limitations to all things. The apostle Paul outlines very specific instructions to the church at Corinth regarding the operation of the marvelous and mighty gifts of the Holy Spirit in public assemblies (more on this later). God's Word establishes protocols which lead to good and godly order and edification, never to confusion and chaos.

I have found there are two important aspects that guide church services as well as church decision-making—government and glory. We must not sacrifice one at the expense of the other. Both are of absolute necessity to fulfill the will of God.

I write now from 50 years of experience and many thousands of ministry engagements regarding the breathtaking and inexplicable aspect of the Holy Spirit's involvement in the framework of our worship services. Great danger to the anointing arises with the advent of the monster of monotony, the cruelty of constancy, and their big brother, boredom. These are deadly transgressions that allow everyone to know exactly what is going to happen before it happens. If we serve Jehovah Bara, God, the Creator of heaven and earth, how is it possible that we have no creativity?

Think of the intricacy of a snowflake and explain to me why dullness and routine must rule Sunday morning. Spontaneity and creativity are the language of the Spirit of Christ. A tremendous hallmark of the charismatic renewal was that more and more churches purged their printed bulletins. They no doubt realized they no longer needed them because everyone had them memorized already. Many mainline churches that depended on liturgical services added less formal services on a weekly basis.

If no two sunrises or sunsets are the same, why should every Sunday church experience follow a rote regimen? It goes something like this: the service opens with three fast songs, followed by two slow songs, and then a chance to worship in the Spirit. Then someone has a message in tongues and someone else interprets—usually in King James English, with all the thees and thous and hasts and wasts included. The speakers are generally always the same individuals. Then there are announcements (*yawn*), then the offering (all but apologized for), then the sermon (often dry-delivered, lacking both compassion and conviction), and finally, some form of altar ministry. Every week, rinse and repeat, with only slight variations.

I understand predictable is safe, but it is also a terrible bore. The cemeteries of churches and marriages, I might add, can attest to that fact. On the other hand, imagine for a moment that you attended a church where you had no idea from one week to the next what was going to take place. You were fully aware that whatever happened was going to be anointed, inspired, and somewhat spontaneous. Most importantly, it would result in people's lives being irreversibly and dramatically changed by God's power. Yet you could never predict what, or with whom, when, or how it was going to happen. I believe your enthusiasm to "not forsake the assembling of yourselves together" (Hebrews 10:25) would significantly increase. I'd say you wouldn't be able to wait to get to church on Sunday, or whenever the doors were open. The creativity and spontaneity of God's Holy Spirit would demonstrably be alive and moving as He did at creation's dawn: "...and the Spirit of God was moving over the surface of the water. God said, 'Let there be light'" (Genesis 1:2-3).

I will deal with the mighty gifts of the Holy Spirit more completely later. I need to announce this now: one of the most exciting things anyone can see in any worship service, as well as in their individual lives, is the unrivaled operation of God's mighty gifts of the Holy Spirit. (The most exciting things is the thrill of witnessing souls being saved.) Many churches and gatherings that purposefully welcome the gifts of the Holy Spirit are also distinguished by the greatest demonstration of signs, wonders, and miracles. This happens both during worship services and among members in their individual lives. If we truly believe that the Holy Spirit is God (and He is) why wouldn't we anticipate and deeply desire for Him to demonstrate His creative power and spontaneous presence among us? Oh, join me and let us pray and plead for it.

All these factors lead to the most essential one of all: a church that relies upon the Holy Spirit will become the most effective in publishing the gospel of Jesus Christ to their community and the world. They will regularly and joyfully bring the Lamb of God slain the reward of His suffering— one more soul born again into His glorious eternal kingdom.

We must recognize that in all good things there is a substantial price to pay for an emphasis on the Holy Spirit. Jesus said as much in John 14:17: "The Spirit of truth, whom the world cannot receive, for it does not see Him, neither does it know Him." Ponder that for a moment. When others see you involving yourself and your family in things for which there simply is no natural explanation, they often become uncomfortable. At times that anxiety can boil over into anger, resentment, even hostility. Accept that they haven't received what you have received, and they can't see Him and don't know Him. They fear what they don't understand. It's not unusual that they may question why you act in some way that seems to have no natural explanation. Even religious people (or I might say especially religious people) do not comprehend why those of us who respect and appreciate the Holy Spirit do so. Because they do not understand it, they are either indifferent to the Holy Spirit, or in some cases may go so far as to oppose His influence.

Another major reason that some in the modern church are resistant to the influence of the Holy Spirit is a reluctance to embrace change. God, the Holy Spirit, will indeed modify, challenge, even overturn our most carefully laid plans—especially when they are at odds with His plans. Following His supernatural leading can be, well, messy. It can for sure become uncomfortable at times. It's difficult for some to come to grips with the fact that the Holy Spirit cannot be categorized, contained, or controlled. He does not fit neatly into liturgies or limitations. Following His direction involves perceived risk. Many folks, including believers, are so averse to risk that they will do anything to avoid it. Unfortunately, this even includes resisting or outright refusing the direction of the Holy Spirit, especially when His direction involves something they perceive as out of the ordinary or unprecedented. They may fear what others will think of them if they take a course of action out of the norm. It is a terrible travesty that social media has afforded us—the desire to be approved by others. I pray that we will become more concerned with God's approval than the accolades of mere humans.

Another factor we cannot ignore is that opposition we may experience from the purveyors of ridicule, accusation, and outright hatred. This should not be surprising. Jesus's words to us from John 15:18-19 are instructive:

> *If the world hates you, you know that it hated Me before it hated you. If you were of the world, the world would love you as its own. But because you are not of the world, since I chose you out of the world, the world therefore hates you.*

There is no benefit to asking why people may hate you. Haters don't need reasons because they do not operate according to reason. They respond according to and at the level of their emotions, with thoughtless obedience to base impulses they do not understand and cannot control. Is it any wonder why violence, depression, suicide, and hate continue to exponentially increase? The Lord Jesus continued this tremendous life lesson a few verses later in John 15:25: "They hated Me without a cause." So square your shoulders, surrender to all that God has for you, and abide under the shadow of the Almighty (Psalm 91). Remember King Jesus's admonition from Revelation 3:16 (KJV), "So then because thou art lukewarm, and neither cold nor hot, I will spue thee out of my mouth."

Here is another living truth to internalize—it's a completely counterproductive activity to attempt to please those who may be critical of you. While it might be nice to have their approval, please realize you do not need their approval to have the approval and blessing of God. Give them no space in your thoughts; never allow anyone to live rent-free in your head. Dr. Lester Sumrall taught me, "Rod, other people's heads are no place to keep your peace and joy."

Let this truth be amplified by Paul's instruction to the church at Ephesus: "Neither give place to the devil" (Ephesians 4:27 KJV). Do not give your tormentors any place. A place is space limited by occupancy, so evict them from your mind. Place also means a position of opportunity so don't give them any opportunity. Anything you do to try to appease them will only open more opportunities for them to become further infuriated and inflamed. It will give them cause to imagine even more outrageous and untrue claims about you. King Jesus gave some kingdom advice for this kind of scenario in Matthew 7:6:

> *Do not give what is holy to the dogs, nor throw your pearls before swine, lest they trample them under their feet and turn around and attack you.*

Christians in general are targets for attack by the unregenerated world, but no group of believers is subject to more bizarre attacks than those who believe in and are recipients of the ministry of the Holy Spirit. That is a small price to pay for God the Holy Spirit's constant presence, protection, and peace!

CHAPTER THREE

THE PENTECOSTAL DISTINCTIVE

With such an abundance of documentation in the canonical book The Acts of the Apostles, or as it is also referred to The Acts of the Holy Spirit, regarding the mighty baptism of the Holy Spirit, it is odd to me that not a small number of modern believers are inimical to the subject. The question is, why do so many either resist or outright deny the infilling and overflowing of the Holy Spirit? There is no single definitive answer. Several reasons become immediately obvious for why the baptism of the Holy Ghost is ignored, overlooked, denied, and even ridiculed by some Christians.

If you were to pose the question, as I have, to current church attenders concerning why miracles are no longer commonplace, most usually shrug and say, "I don't know."

Another response sounds a lot like: "Only Jesus did miracles, because He was God." Then there is always the standard, "We don't need miracles anymore." Let me unpack these answers or excuses in order.

The first one, "I don't know" is probably the most honest of the three. Even a casual reading of the four gospels reveals a plethora of miracles. The volumes of miraculous manifestations continue unabated throughout The Acts of the Apostles, and to a certain extent through the remainder of the New Testament. There, modern churchgoers face a dilemma of doctrine: why are there so many miracles recorded in the Bible, while none are present in their own experience? What is missing? Can anything be done about it? The answers are the baptism of the Holy Ghost—and yes!

A major hindrance to experiencing miracles today is that those who fill our pulpits are silent on the subject. To destroy the church, all that is necessary is for the preacher to become reticent. I have witnessed the mere mention of miracles elicit sheepish embarrassment from pastors. Tragic yet true, I addressed this ministerial bankruptcy of backbone in my book *The Miracles of Jesus*. Here is an excerpt:

> For many in our modern world, the very idea of miracles is ridiculous. They see no need for such a thing, and the thought of actually wanting a miracle is anathema to them. To acknowledge miracles would be an admission that there is a supernatural world, and that would mean they would have to admit the possibility of a supernatural God. And if there was a God, they

would have to decide what to do with Him—to believe in Him, and trust and obey Him, or to reject Him and deal with the consequences of that decision.

The idea of miracles to postmodern man conjures images of chanted incantations and superstitious exercises. But for all their sophistication and information, overindulged moderns are woefully unprepared for conflict, whether it is natural or spiritual. They are in touch with their feelings, but have lost touch with the spiritual aspect of their existence.

In contrast, the man living in a remote region of the world may not know about space flight or the Internet, but he will surely know that there is a spiritual component to his life. He may respond to that knowledge imperfectly, since he many have never heard the gospel message, but he knows that the spirit realm is real and must be reckoned with. Could it be that this man is better positioned to respond to God's intervention than the cosmopolitan urbanite?[9]

This stubborn insistence that miracles—indeed, any supernatural influences—are unnecessary, at least in the Western world, is due to what I have often referred to as our ungodly affluence. As a result, we perceive no need for miracles. After all, we have the best doctors, the finest lawyers, and the most accomplished accountants, as well as an army of others who will meet our needs and cater to our wishes. The idea of miracles, or any form of the supernatural, is therefore dismissed as primitive and old-fashioned notions that are unnecessary and unenlightened.

The second objection in regard to the seeming lack of miracles today involves the Lord Jesus performing miracles because He was God. This assumes that no one else could operate in the miraculous, because obviously they are not God. This response is totally erroneous for a couple of reasons. One is that the Lord Jesus never did anything, miraculous or otherwise, during His earthly ministry exclusively because He was Emmanuel (God with us). He was and is God. The Bible states emphatically from where Christ's ability and propensity to operate in the supernatural came. Here it is in Acts 10:38:

> *How God anointed Jesus of Nazareth with the Holy Spirit and with power, who went about doing good and healing all who were oppressed by the devil, for God was with Him.*

We have no biblical record of the Lord Jesus ever performing miracles previous to being thus anointed for service at John's baptism in the River Jordan (Matthew 3:16). It was only after He received, as a result of the anointing by the Holy Spirit, that He began His mighty ministry confirmed with manifestations of the supernatural.

Here is further verification, from John 14:12; notice that King Jesus did not hesitate and proclaimed boldly: "Truly, truly I say to you, he who believes in Me will do the works that I do also. And he will do greater works than these, because I am going to My Father." First of all, please note the *because*.

Our power is available as a direct result of Jesus returning to His Father and sending the Holy Ghost. The Savior made this statement to His disciples, all of whom were mere men. Therefore, if the only reason Jesus could work miracles was because He was God, He could not legitimately expect His disciples to work them, since they were not God!

The obvious conclusion is that our Lord's miracles were accomplished as a man anointed by the Holy Spirit. He powerfully and prophetically informed His disciples that they could, in fact, do the same works He did (that is, miracles, signs, and wonders) by the same mighty power and authority that enabled Him to do so. That power was the agency and presence of the Holy Ghost.

The Lord Jesus was not the only person who was used with miraculous results in the Bible. The book of The Acts of the Apostles is replete with supernatural incidents, not accomplished by our Savior but by those who believed in Him. Miracles were not limited to the Redeemer in any way. Nor was their scope narrowed to those apostles whom He had chosen. Saul of Tarsus, who became Paul the Apostle, received the restoration of his eyesight after Ananias, an otherwise unknown believer, laid his hands upon him (Acts 9:17-18). Many miracles occurred during a revival in Samaria that began when Philip, the former deacon, went there to proclaim the gospel. This is biblical truth that proves beyond contradiction that miracles were in no way limited to the apostles only.

The third objection I cited in reference to miracles is that they are no longer needed. My response is, "Who says we don't need miracles?" In many churches, they may be rare or extinct, but to say we don't need them is nothing more than presumption or extreme hubris, not to mention selfish. What people are really doing when they voice such a shortsighted rebuttal is that they refuse to consider that God is real and involved in the affairs of men. This is the evil, malignant fruit of secular humanism rotten to its core. However, regardless of how deceived or misinformed one becomes, there can be no escaping the truth that we are spiritual beings. Here is another excerpt from my book *The Miracles of Jesus*:

> I believe it is clear that regardless of how earnestly modern civilization emphasizes the conveniences that technology gives us, we still look for the miraculous. In fact, I believe we need miracles, whether we want to admit it or not. To explain why, I need to direct you to the creation account in the book of Genesis. Genesis 2:7 says: Then the Lord God formed man from the dust of the ground and breathed into his nostrils the breath of life, and man became a living being.
>
> We have been created tripartite beings. The essence of our identity is spirit. We are spirits that have come directly from the Creator. We live in natural bodies, which enable us to remain on the earth, and we possess souls, which enable us to reason, to choose and to feel emotion. But the reality is that we are spirit beings first. That is our true nature, and we cannot deny it. Men may do all kinds of things to camouflage it and cover

it up, to ignore it and ridicule it, but the fact is we are spiritual creatures.

The reason that men have an insatiable curiosity about spiritual things is because God created us as spiritual beings. We need Him to complete us—to fulfill the longing in our hearts for something more than the physical world we live in. We need to know that our lives have value and meaning apart from the number, size or value of all our natural possessions. We may experience pleasure from a proliferation of material things, but true satisfaction and fulfillment can only come from something greater than toys or trinkets, regardless of how much they cost or how impressive they appear.

Manufacturers, retailers and advertisers try to convince people that their lives would be complete if they only had the latest fad or food or feature that they will provide for a fee. But as many materialists have discovered to their dismay, a lot of money does not correlate to a lot of happiness.

In fact, some of the most miserable people alive also have the most money, popularity or notoriety. After having exhausted themselves with amusements, people look for something that is more satisfying. Many become involved with nominally or overtly spiritual pursuits, even those that have nothing to do with God.

There is a horoscope in nearly every newspaper that is published. Fortune tellers do business in every city and community. Board games that actively invite occult activity are perennial favorites. Involvement in cults, witchcraft and Satanism continue to be popular among the rich and famous as well as the poor and unknown.

Drug abuse is rampant among all socioeconomic groups. Many begin dabbling in drugs to see what kind of images they will perceive or experiences they will have under the influence of controlled substances. Before long, they face the deadly specter of addiction, with all the costs and consequences that go along with it. These people are all looking for the supernatural. And in some cases, they find it, but the price they must pay for a glimpse into the dark regions of the spiritual world is high indeed.

Even participation in such innocent hobbies as science fiction, fantasy or horror may be due to a longing to connect with something more meaningful than a life of stultifying sameness. I believe that there is a reason that so many millions worldwide are heading down blind alleys and dead ends while searching for meaning and truth. It is because they are compelled to seek connection with something or someone who can truly assign greater purpose to their lives. That search can only be satisfied in God.[10]

May we plead for more of our great God's involvement and His intervention in our lives, not less. In many cases, divine intervention will occur in the form of miracles or other supernatural manifestations that prove who God is. The miraculous confirms the oversight and involvement of the Almighty in our lives.

Another lightning rod of controversy among believers when it comes to the supernatural is that spiritual things can be falsely attributed with generating divisiveness in the church. During the charismatic renewal, which accelerated in the 1960s, some members of traditional denominational churches happily received the baptism of the Holy Spirit. Those churches were challenged by this development, not because it was unscriptural, but because it created the need for them to examine their long-standing theology.

Local churches and entire organizations became divided about whether the baptism of the Holy Spirit was legitimate. A number affirmed that it was consistent with their doctrine, and others held that it was not. In not a few cases, those who resisted change and desired to maintain the status quo accused those who had received the baptism of the Holy Spirit of causing schism and division.

Quite the opposite was true—those who rejected the validity of the baptism in the Holy Ghost were actually creating the problem. They summarily rejected even the possibility of anyone receiving something from God that did not necessarily mesh with their denominational doctrine or preconceived paradigm. The baptism of the Holy Ghost was regarded as a "new development" within their established ranks. Their position was that those who had received the infilling and overflowing of the Holy Spirit were the instigators and insurrectionists.

The Old Testament is illuminating on this issue in 1 Kings 18. Israel was in the deadly grip of a famine, which had been prophesied by Elijah. Dust, destitution, and the dark specter of death scorched the earth as it thirsted for rain. Ahab and Elijah finally met. First Kings 18:17 tells the story: "When Ahab saw Elijah, Ahab said to him, 'Are you he that troubles Israel?'" Ahab, true to his ungodly nature, attempted to accuse God's prophet of being a troublemaker. After all, Elijah was the one whose words accurately forecast the famine, so it would seem apparent that Ahab was correct. However, that is not the end of the story. Listen to Elijah's riveting response in verse 18:

> *And he answered, "I have not troubled Israel, but you and your father's house, in that you have forsaken the commandments of the Lord and you have followed the Baals."*

Elijah was not responsible for the drought; he had only given heaven's prophetic response to the apostasy and idolatry of Ahab and his regime. Ahab had forsaken and insulted the God of Israel and worshiped another deity. God withheld the rain and announced it by Elijah's prophecy as a consequence. So, as the late, brilliant radio host Paul Harvey would say, "Now you know the rest of the story."

Could it be that rains of God's refreshing and revival have been withheld not because multitudes of God's people are crying out to Him earnestly seeking and desiring everything

He has for them? Isn't the actual problem the attitudes and platitudes of those in places of authority in the church refusing the blessing of the baptism of the Holy Ghost that the living God has for them and for every believer?

Regrettably, this sad scenario has played out in countless churches over the years. There are those who dare to ask for and receive more of Almighty God's promise of power than they have ever been aware of in the past. They begin to understand that there truly is so much more to the Christian life than they have ever been told or that they have ever experienced. God the Holy Spirit floods and fills their entire being to overflowing with Himself. Believers thus empowered, ablaze with the holy fire of God, cannot keep it to themselves. They begin to tell everyone what the Holy Ghost has done in and for them in direct response to exactly what our Bible prophetically declares will happen when we receive the baptism in the Holy Spirit. We become flaming witnesses of the power of God to save, heal, and deliver (Acts 1:8). We must guard against the propensity of those who have not had the same experience rising up to accuse those who have of dividing the church. The issue is not that the baptism of the Holy Spirit is not authentic—but rather because it does not conform to long-standing church dogma. We must never allow the victimizers to blame the victims for the problem without recognizing their own refusal to acknowledge the truth.

This raises another question: is it God's will for every believer to be filled with the Holy Spirit? The answer is undoubtedly and unequivocally, emphatically and absolutely *yes!*

The most common and immediate objection is this, in one form or another: "But you don't have to be baptized with the Holy Spirit to go to heaven!" My response is that you certainly don't—but why wouldn't you want it? What could keep you from desperately desiring and zealously seeking to be filled with the same Holy Spirit who invaded the borrowed tomb of Joseph of Arimathea and raised to life again the three-days-dead body of the Prince of God? To refuse is the denial of three divine directives.

First, according to John the Baptist, part of the purpose of the ministry of the Lord Jesus Christ is to baptize you with the Holy Spirit. The Bible is definitive in Luke 3:16:

> *John answered them all, "I indeed baptize you with water. But One mightier than I is coming, the strings of whose shoes I am not worthy to untie. He will baptize you with the Holy Spirit and with fire."*

How much more directly can it be said? Why would any genuine believer refuse what the Bible so clearly states is a major assignment of our Lord Jesus Christ's purpose in their life? He is the Baptizer with the Holy Ghost. I encourage you at this very moment to open your heart to receive everything God has for you. It is unnatural for any child of God to refuse something sincerely offered to them by our gracious Lord and Savior Jesus Christ. This brings us to the second principle.

I don't know about your home, but in the Parsley household at Christmas or their birthday, our children have always expected something in the form of a gift. How would you feel if, as a parent, you made a great sacrifice to provide your children with a very expensive gift, only to have them ignore it or, even worse, refuse it? What if they said that your gift wasn't necessary or that they wouldn't use it? Imagine if they maintained that they didn't want it, regardless of how costly it was or how difficult it was for you to have obtained? I'm sure you would be devastated at their rejection and distressed by their callous indifference and ingratitude. At the very least, they would appear to be ungrateful.

Those who refuse the baptism of the Holy Spirit must hurt the heart of our benevolent and loving God in much the same way. Oh, the immeasurable, the incomprehensible sacrifice that was made to provide us with the infilling of His Spirit in overflowing measure. May 1 Thessalonians 5:19 (KJV) resound in every humble heart: "Quench not the Spirit."

The third principle we must consider is that our God, Jehovah Jireh (the Lord who provides), has with great purpose provided the glorious baptism of the Holy Spirit to explicitly empower us to fulfill His purpose for our lives in the earth. That purpose is to be a witness of what Jesus Christ has done for us. We are not all called to function as a fivefold ministry office gift of apostle, prophet, evangelist, pastor, or teacher. However, the Holy Spirit will empower each one of us to be supernaturally endowed with extraordinary power. That supernatural power will enable us to accomplish anything and everything He has called us to do, whether that is to stand in front of a classroom full of students or to sit in the driver's seat of a truck. When believers refuse the unmatched benefits of the Holy Spirit's power, they cut themselves off from their supreme and supernatural resources. Those same resources are the ones that are available to help, to comfort, to teach, to guide, to train, to equip them to be more effective at whatever they are called to do in this life! This self-defeating behavior is in many cases unintentional, but we observe it nearly everywhere in the body of Christ. It is difficult to admit, but in my opinion, it is without exception one of the greatest hindrances to world evangelism. It is a major reason why the church has not fulfilled the Great Commission to go into all the world and preach the gospel to every creature (Mark 16:15-20).

Another pervasive objection voiced concerning the baptism of the Holy Spirit stems from those whose doctrine conflates being born again and receiving the baptism of the Holy Spirit. Let me say it with all the emphasis at my disposal— being born again and being filled with the Holy Spirit *are not the same!*

There are several reasons these two experiences are consolidated by well-meaning believers.

First, the confusion seems to stem from similar language being used to describe being born again and being baptized with the Holy Spirit. It is an established fact, and there can be no doubt that the Holy Spirit enters into a person's heart, or spirit, when they are born again (1 John 3:5-8). We are born of the Spirit. However, a careful examination of the language of the Bible will reveal that two separate events are involved.

The two experiences are also equated at times because on one occasion, people were born again and baptized with the Holy Spirit instantaneously, as we see in the case of Cornelius's household in Acts 10. I won't rehearse the entire episode, but the climax, from Acts 10:44-46, says:

> *While Peter was still speaking these words, the Holy Spirit fell on all those who heard the word. All the believers of the circumcision who had come with Peter were astonished, because the gift of the Holy Spirit had been poured out even on the Gentiles. For they heard them speaking in other tongues and magnifying God.*

The people assembled in Cornelius's house were not born again—they were Gentiles, and most Jews didn't believe they could even be saved. This explains their astonishment that the Holy Spirit not only saved them, but also filled them to overflowing, to the point that they spoke in tongues and prophesied. There could be no denying that the Lord God had done an amazing work in their lives—both in being born again, as well as baptized with the Holy Spirit. That the Holy Spirit performed both works instantaneously in no way diminishes the reality of what they had received.

Additional confusion arose in the 19th and early 20th centuries resulting in some groups regarding sanctification as a separate work of grace subsequent to salvation. Many who held this view later became baptized with the Holy Spirit. Many others said the concept of sanctification as separate from salvation was false doctrine and heretical. It was a small step to brand those who went on to receive the baptism of the Holy Spirit—some of whom went so far as to label it as a third work of grace—as heretical also.

Here is scriptural evidence that salvation and the baptism of the Holy Spirit are not one and the same.

First, let's examine the disciples' experience on the Day of Pentecost in Acts 2. Jesus had instructed them to wait in Jerusalem for the promise of the Father. They waited. The Day of Pentecost came, and the Father's promise came, just as the Lord Jesus had said it would. King Jesus had not promised them that they would be born again, since they were saved already. They had previously acknowledged Jesus the Christ as their Savior and Lord before the Day of Pentecost arrived. What they received that day was altogether different. Acts 2:4 enlightens us: "And they were all filled with the Holy Spirit and began to speak in other tongues, as the Spirit enabled them to speak."

This is in no way surprising to us because the Lord Jesus pointed out a distinction in the ministry of the Holy Spirit during His earthly ministry. He encountered the woman at the well outside the city of Samaria as recorded for us in John 4:13-14:

> Jesus said to her, "Everyone who drinks of this water will thirst again, but whoever drinks of the water that I shall give him will never thirst. Indeed, the water that I shall give him will become in him a well of water springing up into eternal life."

John 7:38-39 speaks of water in another form:

"He who believes in Me, as the Scripture has said, out of his heart shall flow rivers of living water." By this He spoke of the Spirit, whom those who believe in Him would receive. For the Holy Spirit was not yet given, because Jesus was not yet glorified.

Water is water wherever it is found, but there is a vast difference between a well of water and rivers of water. In this case, the well of water that is in you refers to being born again. The rivers that flow out of you refer to the baptism of the Holy Spirit. It is the same Spirit, but in a different measure and for a different purpose. The well of water refers to an individual believer's salvation. The rivers of water refer to a believer's witness to the surrounding world.

In Acts 19, we are told that the apostle Paul encountered a group of believers in Ephesus. He asked them in verse 2, "Have you received the Holy Spirit since you believed?" If being born again of the Spirit was the same as receiving the baptism of the Holy Spirit, why would Paul, who would certainly have understood the distinction or the lack thereof, ask them, "Have you received the Holy Spirit *since* you believed?" The result was that these believers received something supernatural that was subsequent to and different from their salvation. If they had not been saved at this point, Paul would have surely known it and would not have framed his question as he did.

Finally, a biblical explanation of the distinction between salvation and the baptism of the Holy Spirit is found in Acts

8, during the great revival in the city of Samaria. Here is the narrative, from Acts 8:5,12:

> *Philip went down to the city of Samaria and preached Christ to them. ...But when they believed Philip preaching about the kingdom of God and the name of Jesus Christ, both men and women were baptized.*

At this point it should be clear that the people in Samaria heard the gospel and were born again. If there is doubt here, just listen to the words of Jesus in Mark 16:16: "He who believes and is baptized will be saved. But he who does not believe will be condemned." According to Acts 8:12, the men and women of Samaria believed and were baptized. According to no less an authority than the Lord Jesus Christ Himself, these Samaritans were saved. Watch what happens next. Acts 8:14-17 explains:

> *Now when the apostles who were at Jerusalem heard that Samaria had received the word of God, they sent Peter and John to them. When they came down, they prayed for them that they might receive the Holy Spirit, for still He had come on none of them. They were only baptized in the name of the Lord Jesus. Then they laid their hands on them, and they received the Holy Spirit.*

The apostles at Jerusalem fully understood the distinct difference between salvation and the baptism of the Holy Spirit. That was the exact purpose for which they sent Peter and John to the city—so that the believers there could also receive the mighty baptism of the Holy Spirit. If they were one and the same, there would be no need for Peter and John to go there at all.

The Bible makes it abundantly clear that the baptism of the Holy Spirit is an experience available to a born again believer subsequent to their salvation. There is no scriptural evidence that the baptism of the Holy Spirit was only offered to a certain group, or for any specified time period. It is the promise of God for all of His children. It is unparalleled; I know from personal experience. I will tell you about that next.

CHAPTER FOUR

ACCESSING THE SUPERNATURAL: THE SPARK OF POWER

By God's amazing grace and faith in Jesus Christ, I was wonderfully born again when I was but eight years of age. My family had always been members of the Freewill Baptist denomination, and we were deeply devoted to the proclamation of the gospel of Christ and the advancement of His kingdom. It was the very centerpiece of our lives. My parents volunteered their time, their financial support, and effort to our local church every week. We attended every service, Sunday morning, Sunday night, and Wednesday night, as well as revival services that would sometimes run for weeks at a time. We never missed church that I can remember.

As an eight-year-old, I certainly didn't have the knowledge of God that I acquired in later years. However, I knew that I didn't want to spend eternity separated from God and my family in hell. I understood that receiving Jesus Christ as my personal Savior was the only way to avoid that outcome.

I went with my parents and sister to a revival meeting being held in a small and meager concrete block building where a woman was preaching. Our church did not believe in women preachers at the time, but we always supported any church in our area that was attempting to win souls. We were always hungry for the presence of God, so we attended. The altar call for salvation was given at the close of a fiery message of gospel preaching. As I remember, I was the only one who responded. Those few but anointed people prayed with me as I publicly accepted Jesus Christ as my personal Savior and Lord. Afterward, the mighty lady preacher asked me how I felt. I replied, "I feel like I have just had a bath on the inside." I had no chapter and verse explanation, but that was pretty good theology! (See Psalm 51:1-10.)

The kind of bath I was referencing was not a luxurious bubble bath with a Dove beauty bar. What was in my eight-year-old mind was a bath in a number-two galvanized wash-tub with lye soap and a towel that was one step removed from sandpaper. By the way, lye soap gets you clean by removing the first three layers of your skin—that's clean, friend! I was genuinely born again, and I had become a new creature (2 Corinthians 5:17). I am thankful for the convicting and convincing power of the Holy Ghost and the saving grace of faith in Jesus Christ. I have never regretted for a single moment the commitment I made that night, and it is as real today as it was nearly 60 years ago.

From that time until now, I've always been drawn to preachers. As a child, more often than not, after a church service I would go up to them (they were accessible then) and wrap my arms around their legs while they stood in the foyer greeting folks as they left the building. I had no thought that I would ever become a pastor, but I always wanted to be around them, regardless of where they were or what they were doing.

In my teenage years, I began to notice and have questions about things that didn't seem to occur to me when I was younger. I loved God more than ever, and I desired with all of my heart to be pleasing to Him and to live faithful to His word. Two issues in particular troubled me.

The first was what I perceived as discrepancies between what my church taught and what my Bible said. Our preachers were godly and wonderful men who proclaimed the gospel of Christ without compromise. The people we fellowshipped with were our family members, friends, and acquaintances who all genuinely loved God and desired deeply to do His will. However, there were certain things that we adhered to that didn't seem to be in agreement with what I encountered as I continued to read and study the Bible.

There was the matter of dress—specifically, women's dress. It seemed to me that women were being singled out by having special restrictions placed upon them. Women's clothing had to be modest (with this, I remain in agreement)—although what constituted modesty was not specifically defined. Pants, short skirts, open-toed shoes, and necklines anywhere much lower than chin level were all either outright forbidden or frowned upon. Heavy makeup was equated to a lack of holiness and loose living. Although most men who could afford them wore suits to church, there were fewer restrictions placed upon them. It seemed to me that any attempt women could make to improve their appearance was regarded as improper.

As I came to understand later, holiness has much less to do with how we appear on the outside than with the attitudes and convictions of our heart on the inside (1 Samuel 16:7). I am certainly in stark disagreement with the current culture's emphasis on exposing oneself, but I felt that the so-called clothesline sermons of that time went too far.

Another issue that arose was the church's limitations on which forms of entertainment were acceptable. Trends in fashion, film, television, music, and athletics, especially, while not always expressly forbidden, were tightly regulated. Keep in mind that I was coming of age during a time when every restriction was being re-evaluated and many were rebelled against. For men, allowing your hair to grow over your ears was seen to be an act of rebellion. What was a fashion choice by a young person was often regarded as defiance by their elders, creating unnecessary conflict.

Traditional church music was experiencing influence by new types of worship. Drums, guitars, and tambourines began to be used beside or in place of pianos, organs, and harps. Hymns were supplemented and then supplanted in many places by worship songs and scripture choruses in what was referred to as Jesus music—now known as contemporary Christian music.

Younger believers chafed under the restrictive atmosphere of traditional churches and chose to leave as a result. Some returned later, but for many the exit was permanent. My default setting was to always stay with God and with His church. However, I recognized a restlessness and dissatisfaction with the, at times, rather stale Christian life I saw and experienced.

I was also struggling with the daunting matter of a career. I realize now that our culture places a great deal of pressure on young people to decide what direction the rest of their lives will take long before they are ready to tackle such a question. I assumed I would be enrolling in college, but I was totally perplexed about what course of study I should pursue. I had always wanted to do something meaningful with my life—something that helped others and therefore glorified my Savior. I reasoned that the practice of law might be a way to accomplish those goals. Two things developed that completely changed my perspective.

Like many baby boomers, the dissatisfaction in general that I was experiencing with the state of my Christian life caused me to seek after something more. Please understand the *more* I was seeking was always within the boundaries of Christianity. I never entertained the thought of my search ever extending to other religions, cults, or spiritual pursuits such as new age or witchcraft. I didn't dabble in drugs, alcohol, or sexual sin—three influences that were (and still are) used by satan to destroy millions of lives.

I saw miracles in the Bible, but they weren't common in my life. We prayed that people would be healed in our church, but our prayers always included the escape clause "if it be thy will." I heard people talk about a deeper life with God, but I could only guess what that meant. I prayed. I read my Bible. I went to every church service I could in search of anything that would answer the gnawing need for more of God's presence. What I saw in His Word burned in my soul. I wasn't satisfied or convinced that I had everything God promised me. I was driven to discover everything available to me through His glorious grace.

It was my habit in those days to scour the local newspaper (does anyone remember those?) for advertisements about revivals and church meetings. I came across a notice of such a church service hosting a speaker who had spent time in concentration camps as a young boy during World War II. The church was quite close to my home, so I prepared to attend. I was intrigued by the prospect of hearing from someone who had firsthand experience of surviving the horrors of Hitler's death camps. I noticed that the church where he was scheduled to speak was known as a full gospel church. I was unsure what that meant, but that didn't deter me. If they had God, I wanted more of Him in whatever measure I could find. What I discovered was far greater than anything I had expected.

The worship service was like none I had ever experienced. There were over 1,000 people in attendance. They were all standing, and hundreds of them were young people. Many ethnicities and socioeconomic backgrounds were represented. Suddenly, at the close of a scripture chorus, the congregation with hearts, heads, and hands uplifted began to sing. I had never heard such harmonious, spontaneous, heartfelt singing in my life. It was heavenly, angelic, and celestial. It reverberated, swelled then subsided, and then swelled again. The worshipers' faces seemed to glow with joy. Tears of adulation and adoration were flowing. I stood spellbound because I could not understand a single word they were singing. I learned later it was the language of the Holy Spirit. Then, almost as involuntarily as it had begun, it ended.

There was a moment of silence, and then a man on the platform began to speak again. His words were unintelligible to me. As soon as his unknown syllables concluded, another gentleman began speaking in English with the words, "Thus says the Lord." I would learn later these were two gifts of the Holy Spirit, tongues and interpretation of tongues (more on these gifts in Chapter Seven). I was awestruck, weeping while smiling, submerged in the holy presence of God as I never before knew was possible this side of heaven.

Dr. Bill Basansky's message that night was deeply inspiring. He closed with an altar call for salvation. Out of deep respect for those responding, I stayed, as I had been taught, thinking that would be the conclusion of this extraordinary service. I was wrong! After praying for those who had accepted Christ as Savior—and there were many —the speaker then made another appeal. He invited anyone who wanted to be filled with the Holy Spirit to come forward for prayer.

I had heard about the baptism of the Holy Spirit, both in positive and negative terms. Since the church of my upbringing did not include it in their doctrine, what little I had heard about the subject was incomplete and speculative. Now I needed to make a choice. If I really wanted more of God, and I did, I felt that whatever I witnessed in that service had to be key. This was my opportunity. On the other hand, no one I knew had experienced this, so I was without an example to follow about what it was or what kind of effect it would have. I had come to the service alone, so I had no one to consult about my decision. I deliberated about what to do for a few moments. My initial reluctance was overcome by my overwhelming desire to receive what I witnessed from God in those people that night. I found myself walking to the altar.

Dr. Basansky was very gracious and patient in explaining what was about to take place. He shared about the Day of Pentecost in Acts 2 and said that same experience was available to everyone who had trusted Christ as Savior. He then led us in a short prayer asking the Lord Jesus to fill us with the Holy Spirit. He said he would pray for us individually, and according to God's Word, we would receive the baptism of the Holy Ghost and the ability to speak in other tongues or pray in the Holy Spirit.

As he came closer to me, I could hear those who had received begin speaking in a language I could not understand and had never heard before. I can't describe exactly how it felt when I was prayed for. It was like the most pure joy I'd ever been blessed to sense bubbling up and flowing in streams from the deepest part of my existence. Then its release was flowing from my mouth and vocal cords as I began speaking in a language my mind did not comprehend—but my heart felt those words and my ears heard those words. I felt the greatest connection to the Spirit of God and to eternal reality I had ever known.

I did not completely understand the entire experience, but I knew that it was from God. I had an indescribable awareness of peace and well-being. I knew beyond all fear of contradiction that at last I had discovered the *more* I had been so desperately seeking. I continued to worship, speaking in tongues. Time became inconsequential to me. After what felt to me to be a few minutes, the custodian came to me and said it was time to close the church building. I had lingered, being overwhelmed by the very presence of the living God at that altar speaking in that heavenly language for nearly three hours' time.

I actually don't remember driving home. A whole new world of possibility had burst open to me. However, I was unsure what to do next. I had a thousand questions. The God in Christ had become the Christ in me. I was so exhilarated and so animated that I rushed to tell my parents. Finding them asleep, it was my exuberant joy to awaken them and share my news! They were happy for me, but had as little understanding about the baptism of the Holy Spirit as I had prior to that night. I reluctantly went to bed, but in no way could I begin to fall asleep as my Savior's presence was still lingering and tangible. Just a few hours before sunrise, I drifted off. I was a junior in high school.

I began searching to find and study everything I could about the baptism of the Holy Spirit. I was unable to speak about it to my pastor, since it was not a doctrine of our denomination. Still, I persisted in my exploration, convinced that my baptism in the Holy Ghost was an enormously significant key in my pursuit of God.

During that time, I was confused on another front. It seemed that every time I would take any kind of step in the direction of fulfilling my desire to pursue my education, I would become ill. I would have physical symptoms without any evidence of their cause. I was now graduated from high school and seemingly on pause as to further pursuits, be it career or college.

Something was wrong. I had been restless and troubled for some time. I attempted to busy myself in order to block it out or push it away, but it could not and would not be denied. It affected my eating, my sleep, and my interactions with others, resulting in an attack on my health and general well-being. The crisis was acute and finally came to a strategic inflection point. I was in the car with my mother headed yet again to another appointment with another physician.

She expressed her concern over the uncertainty of the cause of my distress. She mentioned the possibility of my being admitted to the hospital to undergo a series of tests. Suddenly and without previous thought I shouted, "I know what's wrong with me!"

She responded, "If that's the case, you'd better be telling us, because your condition is serious."

I said, "Maybe I'm called to preach!" And just as quickly and emphatically I retorted, "No, I'm not; I have no idea why I would say that. I've never even considered that."

If there was anyone I knew who could be trusted with that revelation, it was my mother. Although she was driving, and it seemed like her only son may have stripped a gear, she didn't slam on the brakes or run us into a ditch. She looked straight ahead and said in a simple yet stern tone, "Well, if you're called to preach, first be sure you're called of God and no one else; and second, you need to go to college and prepare yourself." I found the closest Bible college to our home and enrolled the next semester.

In the meantime, I accomplished attending real estate school and obtaining my license while also working a construction job. A former childhood pastor of mine heard about my intention to study for the ministry. He graciously invited me to preach on a Sunday night. I studied as if I was preparing for the state bar exam. Finally, the day arrived, I was introduced (that didn't take long), and I stepped to the pulpit as if I knew exactly what I was doing. I preached everything I had prepared, and everything else that came to my mind. My inaugural message lasted exactly 17 minutes. I turned to the pastor and said, "Well, that's all I have to say," and sheepishly retired to my seat.

The pastor arose and took my place at the pulpit and said, "Well, thank you, Brother Parsley. Praise God!" I never really knew whether he was relieved that I was finished so quickly or that he was genuinely thanking God that he'd given me the opportunity to preach so I could get it out of my system and not quit my day job. Whichever way he meant it, I'm sure we were both sincerely gratified that it was over. I am forever in the debt of the godly people of that church who welcomed and so wonderfully encouraged me at such a pivotal time in my young life.

In a few weeks I was off to Bible college. During my sophomore year, the school approached me about the possibility of joining their student traveling gospel trio as a preacher. They would sing and I would bring a message during engagements at churches in their denomination. I was eager for the experience, so I jumped at the opportunity.

Before we set out on our first ministry trip, I was called to the president's office. He was a wonderful and loving man whom I admire to this day. He asked, "We've heard that you're…well, you know, a charismatic, is that right?"

"Yes, sir," I said.

"You know we don't believe in that, don't you?"

"Yes sir, I am aware of that," I said.

He replied, "Well, we just need you to say that you don't really believe that in order for you to remain in the group. Are you willing to do that?" I shared with him that I was sure he didn't actually want me to do such a thing; that it would be unconscionable for me to deny what God had done for me.

Needless to say, I didn't travel with the group but remained very happily enrolled at, and eventually graduated from, that very fine institution.

Near the end of my sophomore year, two friends of our family approached me with a request.

"We know you are in Bible college," they said. "We want to learn more about the Bible. Would you be willing to teach us?"

They wanted to grow in their knowledge of God's Word. I was in Bible college and studying God's Word and training for ministry. It sounded great. I could sharpen my skills, they would learn some new things, and the commitment would last for a few weeks. Since warmer weather was approaching, I could use the backyard picnic shelter my father had built to hold the meetings. I agreed, so we set a day and time.

The day of the Bible study arrived. The ladies drove up to our home and got out. Then another car arrived, and another, and another. Before long, 17 people were assembled to hear what I had to say from God's Word. Twelve of them were my extended family members; only five were not. The guests must have been pleased, because they asked if we could do it again the following week. Weeks went by, and the group continued to grow.

My mother had started her own real estate brokerage firm. Her brother (my uncle) and I had received our real estate licenses at the same time, and we were covering an open house. We were discussing the success of the Bible study. He leaned across the card table where we were sitting in that empty house and said, "I think we should start a church."

I didn't know anything about starting a church or being a pastor. I was a Bible college student. However, I wasn't bashful. I was confident that God had called me and my family would help me.

My enthusiastic response was, "Why not? Let's do it!" We began making plans to launch a new local church. To everyone's surprise, it became immediately greatly blessed and continued to grow. We were forced to change locations several times to find a space that would seat the increasing congregation. We finally were favored to obtain a lease on a warehouse space below a bar in a strip mall—certainly an auspicious portent of things to come! From there we purchased a five-acre parcel of vacant land and built our first building seating 180 people in 1979—mostly by volunteer labor. It was white, sat atop a hill with windows on the sides, steps ascending to the front door, and a steeple with a bell that we rang every Sunday morning. We had an organ, a piano, a pulpit, and a choir loft. I felt like Billy Graham!

The new church required so much of my time and effort that I had to make the decision to let my college enrollment lapse. I felt I could get back to it before much time passed. (As I mentioned, I did finish my degree program there—30 years later.) But something else became an unforeseen crisis that required more of us than we could have ever imagined.

God graced me with one sibling, a sister named Debbie who was two years my elder. She was married about the time I enrolled in Bible college. Within a few months, to her immeasurable delight, she discovered she was pregnant. One unforgettable day in the eighth month of her pregnancy, her husband became ill, so Debbie went to a pharmacy to pick up some over-the-counter medication that would give him some relief. It was raining heavily, and water had accumulated in a large puddle on the road. Her car hydroplaned, causing her to lose control. She went over an embankment and crashed head-on into a concrete barrier. The force of the accident broke her hip and impaled her femur bone into her womb.

The medical staff in the emergency room gave her the grim findings. She would need to undergo immediate emergency surgery to remove her baby and repair her hip. There was no alternative. She begged them for a moment alone. They left her room. When they returned, she was adamant. She refused to allow them do anything that could possibly result in bringing harm to her baby. She agreed they would perform a C-section when the baby was at term.

The doctors who had examined her were dismayed. They remonstrated with my sister. They cautioned her of the possible outcomes, including that both she and her baby could lose their lives. She was unmoved. She endured unending, excruciating pain for weeks until her miracle baby girl, Amy, was born by natural childbirth!

By this time, her hip had become unrepairable and would have to be replaced, but even that option could not guarantee success. This began an endless round of emergency room visits, hospital stays, and surgical procedures. Finally, Debbie was sent home with unlimited prescriptions for several kinds of opioid painkillers and a prognosis of three months to live. She unfortunately became addicted to the medications, and spiraled downward in what seemed to be an unending cycle of doom. We searched for answers anywhere we hoped they might be found.

A wonderful friend, Ron Dailey, told us about a Bible teacher named Norvel Hayes who was known for great faith and the miracles that were quite numerous in his ministry—especially with people who were regarded as hopeless cases. He was conducting a series of services in a hotel ballroom in

Indianapolis, Indiana, a four-hour drive from our home. We loaded Debbie in a vehicle and made our way from Columbus for the weekend meeting.

It was not simply a matter of attending the meetings to learn more of God's Word and enjoy His presence. We were beyond desperate. She was dying. Most days and nights were, in brief, a nightmarish hell on earth. My sister was living in absolute agony. Our assignment was daunting. She was bound to bed or a wheelchair and was half out of her mind with pain and in an opioid-induced stupor. We were aware that it would be impossible for her to sit in a chair for hours at a time. She was vehemently opposed to going in the first place. At one point, I was able to pull her frail body back into the SUV as she had attempted to jump out the door. It took a herculean effort just to get her into the building.

Our friends who had invited us were also leading worship for Brother Hayes. They explained our situation and graciously introduced our family to him. In the course of one of the services, Brother Hayes invited those who were in need of healing to the altar. He then asked for me to join him on the platform. I was shocked. As I was approaching him, he told the congregation that I was a young Baptist preacher from Ohio and that we had come for prayer for my sister. He then asked the people to shout, "Thank God Debbie is healed" several times. Well, I thought, why would he say such a thing? I turned to see if something had taken place of which I was unaware. Nope, there she was in her chair, chin on her chest, passed out!

Brother Hayes, to my utter dismay said, "Come here, Rob." (He said Rob, with a b.)

My friend whispered in his ear, "His name is Rod, not Rob."

Brother Hayes laughed and replied, "I don't care what his name is, I just want his hands."

For what? He proceeded to announce, "Now watch, people. God's going to use this young Baptist preacher to lay hands on all these people so they can be healed." What? I had no clue what "lay hands on" even meant!

Brother Hayes very patiently took me over to the first person standing in the line facing the pulpit area. "Here's what I want you to do," he said. "Just take your fingers and very gently—very gently, put them on their forehead." He took my hand in his and demonstrated what I should do. When my fingers touched the first person's forehead, the entire line of people fell like dominoes to the floor as though they had all passed out! I was undone. I had never seen or heard of anything like it before. I wouldn't have believed it if I hadn't seen it for myself.

Many more supernatural events took place during that series of services. Those three days became an introductory intensive training course for me in this ministry of the Holy Spirit and His gifts that would indelibly mark my ministry.

We were witnessing others at the meetings being instantly healed and delivered. But we were in deep, dark despair for Debbie to be set free and healed from her dependence on prescription medication. In the last few months, she had also resorted to mixing the drugs with hard liquor. It was the last service and our minds raced. What would happen if we returned home with Debbie in the same heart wrenching, deplorable condition? We attempted to be brave in the middle of the sheer terror of losing her. Brother Hayes asked us to bring Debbie to the altar. We managed to roll her chair into place.

He spoke to the group, "This is Debbie. Tonight we're going to pray for her to be set free." He led all those gathered in prayer for her.

Debbie became very animated and agitated and began to forcefully resist our efforts to keep her in place. Brother Hayes wrapped his arms around her and began to pray for her personally. She attempted to loose herself from his grasp, and the ill-tempered scowl on her face became grotesquely, demonically distorted. I no longer recognized my own sister. The whites of her eyes became a hideous reddish-green, her pupils almost cat-like. Her skin was cold to the touch and had the gray tone of death. If Brother Hayes had not held on to her so tightly, I believe by the power of the Holy Ghost, she would have become uncontrollable.

Through it all, Brother Hayes and the many students from his Bible college in attendance never stopped praying and interceding. I had never witnessed such determination as they boldly declared her deliverance. At one point, her damaged leg was raised behind her to a horizontal position from the hip. Two men joined me in a vain attempt to push it back to its normal position. Supernatural, sinister forces were striving to tear my sister out of Brother Hayes' grasp.

She was screaming, "Don't let them take me!" over and over. Just when it seemed like an endless standoff, Debbie's shrieks changed to, "No! I won't go with you! These people love me! I won't go with you!" Her leg returned to its normal place and her foot again rested on the floor. Her rigid body relaxed as she began to weep. Her eyes became normal and bright, her face no longer contorted. As my precious sister returned to us, she turned to me and with tears asked, "Where am I? What happened?"

I hugged her and said, "Welcome home." The name of the Lord Jesus Christ and the supernatural and miraculous power of the Holy Ghost of Pentecost had set her free. Her pain had abated. She was in her right mind and able to think clearly and feel normal.

Brother Hayes had held her in his arms, praying, refusing to allow "them" to have her for two hours and 45 minutes' time. It was the single greatest miracle of deliverance I have ever witnessed, and in 50 years of gospel ministry, I have seen a multitude of them. It will never be erased from my memory. It is forever branded upon my heart by the flaming finger of the Holy Ghost of Pentecost. Nor will I ever cease to thank and glorify the Lord Jesus Christ for Brother Norvel Hayes's intrepid determination to see Debbie snatched from death and set at liberty.

My sister had been given up by medical doctors, having done all they could do. She was sent home to die with only three months to live. Let me testify—my only sibling went on to live, and pray, and prevail for another 30 years before she was gloriously received into the loving arms of King Jesus and entered her eternal reward in heaven.

By the time that Saturday evening service had closed, it was far into the morning hours of Sunday. We drove home transformed forever and energized by all that we had been graced to see and experience. I went directly to our little 180-seat fledgling church and changed my clothes in my tiny office. As soon as the music portion of our service had ended, I stood in the pulpit to share the testimony of the Holy Ghost's deliverance of my sister, Debbie. I prophetically proclaimed to the overflowing congregation: "From this day forward, whatever you see happen in Matthew, Mark, Luke, or John and the book of Acts of the Apostles in your Bible is not only possible, it is entirely probable and likely to happen in this church. If you are in need of divine healing or a miracle, get to this altar."

People filled every aisle and, like a wave, rushed toward the front. At that time, there were two rows of pews in the building with an aisle on each side and one in the middle. The Holy Ghost ushered them to the front of the center aisle, they began to fall to the floor under the mighty Pentecostal power of God. Remember now, we were a Baptist church! I did not even get the opportunity to lay hands on any of them. The same Holy Spirit who fell on the first Pentecost recorded in the book of Acts was being poured out without measure upon a Baptist congregation in a 180-seat white chapel in a cornfield in Ohio! We were all receiving the touch of God for whatever we needed without any human intervention at all. Soon there was such a pile of people in the aisles that others coming forward were unable to get anywhere close to the front, and God met them wherever they were. Everything and everyone was forever changed by the mighty rushing wind of God's Holy Spirit that day. It was as glorious as it was unprecedented in our newly launched church.

That chapter in my life became my introduction to the supernatural aspects of Pentecostal ministry. It had a profound and enduring effect upon me, my family, and on what became World Harvest Church. Salvations, signs, wonders, and miracles became commonplace. People enthusiastically shared about what they were experiencing. Those who heard their firsthand testimonies began to attend our services to behold the Holy Ghost outpouring for themselves. As a result, our church enjoyed an entire series of explosive growth cycles.

One notable miracle that occurred during those early days involved a precious lady who had been diagnosed with advanced osteoporosis. As a result of the disease, her bones became very brittle and fragile. At an early age, she was confined to a wheelchair due to multiple fractures, and it was extremely difficult for her to perform even the simplest tasks. We prayed for her in one of our services after she and her wheelchair were carried into the building by our ushers. Shortly afterward, she returned to church without her wheelchair. She had been gloriously healed in the name of Jesus Christ and the triumphant power of Pentecost; her broken bones were supernaturally mended together. All of her casts, braces, and bandages were gone, to the glory of God!

God enabled us to double the size of our original building to 400 seats. One and half years later were forced to build a larger adjacent 1,200-seat building to accommodate the crowds. Even with the increased capacity, we still had to host multiple services. Remember, this was in the late 1970s and early 1980s when no one had ever heard of multiple services. We were of necessity conducting five gatherings every week. Within a very short time—less than ten years by God's grace and the constant presence and demonstration of the Holy Ghost—our congregation grew supernaturally. We went from 17 people to constructing a 5,200-seat tabernacle, as well as offices, a television studio, a K-12 Christian school, and children's church classrooms.

Thanks be to God, the miracles have never stopped since those very early days of World Harvest Church nearly 50 years ago. The unquestionable key to it all has been a willingness to receive all that God's Word promises, including and of utmost necessity the mighty baptism of the Holy Spirit. I cannot possibly imagine what ministry or life would be like without the blessing of the Holy Ghost. I believe it has been a paramount, fundamental principle of God's kingdom in my life. It has enabled both me personally and the church it is my privilege to have founded and continue to pastor to be effective in proclaiming the gospel of Jesus Christ throughout our community, our nation, and the world.

CHAPTER FIVE

THE ANTIDOTE FOR THE MODERN CHURCH AND CULTURE

There are strident voices in the Christian world that have derided those who affirm the baptism of the Holy Spirit as uneducated bumpkins who need some kind of miraculous intervention in order to maintain their faith. Others, as I have mentioned before, hold that miracles and the means for acquiring them are unnecessary for various reasons. Still others maintain that expecting the miraculous is tantamount to superstition or other debunked religious myths. I find it interesting that most of this brand of ridicule emanates from those labeled as religious leaders in Western culture. In other parts of the world, Pentecostal churches are among the largest and fastest growing.

According to the World Christian Encyclopedia, when I was born in 1957, there were 10 million Pentecostals in the world. By 1982, that number had swelled to 51 million. In 2023, there were 644 million Pentecostals/Charismatics in the world, making this the fastest-growing group in the Christian world.[11]

The baptism of the Holy Spirit has certainly not been kept secret nor is it fading away. In fact, its influence and its adherents are dramatically increasing. Could it be that this multiplication is because it is even more necessary now than ever?

My pastor and mentor Dr. Lester Sumrall said, "The church is responsible for the well-being of the country. As the church goes, so goes the nation." His words were never more accurate and appropriate than they are today. A casual glance at the current condition of our culture indicates that the church at large and the nation as a whole are in desperate need of God's Holy Spirit capable of producing a dynamic direction or shift. Here are some stark and startling statistics.

According to the Religious Freedom Index, of Americans in general, 59 percent say that religion is a *part of the solution* to problems. Among Generation Z (those between 12 and 27 years old in 2024), 61 percent say religion is the *source* of all problems! It gets worse—64 percent say a person should not be free to preach their faith to others. Only 38 percent say that it is acceptable to view marriage as only between one man and one woman. We are not in danger of losing a generation—we have already lost them, and without Holy Ghost intervention, we will never get them back.

This is why. For the most part, what a person believes by age 13 is what they will die believing. The church has essentially a ten-year window to influence people with the gospel—from the ages of 4 to 14. Ninety million of the 300 million people in America are between those ages right now. Eighty percent of those 90 million children *never* go to church. Four of five church leaders in America today grew up in church. Unless something changes in a dramatic fashion, we won't have any church leaders left a generation from now.

For that matter, without a Holy Spirit-inspired, culture-transforming awakening, we may see the church in America declining to an all-time historic low. Even now, church attendance is down. The number of churches is down. Passion for evangelism is down. One major evangelical denomination had the lowest number of baptisms they have recorded for over 100 years. This is scarcely surprising, since two-thirds of churches have no evangelism training available whatsoever. Fifty-one percent of evangelicals have never heard the great commission.[12] I suspect that if they have heard the words, they have no idea of its significance or how to accomplish it. Ninety-five percent of believers will never win one single soul to Christ in their lifetime.[13] While 82 percent of the unchurched are at least somewhat likely to attend church if invited, only 2 percent of church members invite a single unchurched person to church each year. No wonder, then, that 50 percent of churches will not add one person to their ranks in two years' time.[14]

It takes 100 churches spending $100,000 to win one soul in the United States, which has now become the fourth largest mission field in the world. Churches in America have spent three trillion dollars in the last ten years and have no statistically significant growth to show for it. Eighty-five percent of churches in the United States are in decline. Whatever we have been doing has been spectacularly and stupendously ineffective. I would give us an A for activity, but a failing grade for results. Surely this is not what God intended when He received the Lord Jesus back into heaven and dispatched the mighty Holy Spirit to endue us with His power that we might propagate His glorious gospel (Matthew 28:18-22; Acts 1:8).

And if, by some miracle, a poor struggling sinner makes their way to a church, the question looms—what is he or she going to find when they get there? According to the Family Research Council and George Barna's survey of churchgoing Americans, less than half of all believers live according to orthodox Christian beliefs. Only 47 percent of believers affirm that when you die you go to heaven only because of repenting of your sin and accepting Christ as Savior. Fifty-three percent believe that there are many ways to heaven. Fifty-nine percent do not believe that humans are born in sin and can only be saved from sin's consequences through faith in Jesus Christ. Fifty-two percent believe that there are no moral absolutes.

Let me make the case for a fresh baptism of Pentecostal power even more clearly. Among evangelicals, 75 percent come to know Jesus as Savior before they are 18 years old. Eleven percent come to faith between the ages of 18 and 24. Only 8 percent are saved between the ages of 25 and 34. A mere 6 percent of Christians receive salvation after the age of 35. The chances of someone being born again after age 65 are one in 750,000. The average age when people accept Jesus as Savior is 12.

It seems clear to me that while we must preach the gospel of Christ to every age group, we should be focusing major efforts on children and young people. Think of it in these terms. If a corporation was responsible for selling a product, and it spent the vast majority of its time and finances focused on the demographic that was least likely to purchase their merchandise, that company would soon be bankrupt. Yet in most instances the American church continues blindly operating exactly as it always has, with little or no concern for instituting the necessary course corrections.

We must realize that there are deeply systemic problems in our modus operandi. To solve our deficiency will require much more than a slight tweak in programs and techniques that haven't worked for years, and sometimes decades. In short, we need a complete Holy Ghost overhaul of our priorities. We have need of a revolution in our visionary thinking and planning. It's time to ask God for wisdom and the blessed Holy Ghost of Pentecost for direction and empowering strategies and the heart of the Lord Jesus Christ to release us into a new paradigm.

Remember the purpose of Pentecost was first and foremost to spread the gospel to the entire world. It is certainly true that this generation has advantages that no other generation before has enjoyed regarding the ability to promote and spread the gospel of Calvary's Lamb worldwide. We must full well embrace these advantageous opportunities. As few as three of these advantages alone should provide us with the means necessary to fulfill Matthew 24:14: "And this gospel of the kingdom will be preached throughout the world as a testimony to all nations, and then the end will come."

First among these is *transportation*. Ships in ancient times were quite limited in possible routes and destinations, due to navigation complications. With few exceptions, much of their travel was along coastlines or within sight of land. Instruments such as the compass became essential as navigation aids. Other beneficial developments included the sextant, which made determinations of latitude more precise. Later, reliable chronometers finally gave mariners a way to calculate their longitude as well as latitude, making navigation much more accurate and efficient. But it was not until the middle of the 20th century that air travel began to supplant ships for travel from one place to another worldwide with ease. A tip of the hat goes to fellow Ohioans, Wilbur and Orville Wright, for inventing the first airplane that flew its maiden flight of 120 feet on December 17, 1903.

However, feet have historically been the most common way for people to move about on land. All praise to our Creator Jehovah Bara for creating us *imageo dei* (in the image of God). The wheel, invented in modern day Iraq in the fourth millennium B.C., was revolutionary in its ability to assist movement. Horses have also been used from antiquity. Thomas Newcomen is credited with creating the steam engine in 1712, which started things moving by railroad travel. And the first commercially successful internal combustion engine, invented by a Belgian named Etienne Lenoir around 1860, led to the rise of automobiles. This gave the masses access to transportation unknown and unimagined by those in previous ages, including my favorite, a 1957 Chevy Bel Air—thanks Etienne!

Today, it is possible for most people to go to an airport, usually a short distance from their homes, and within a day or less be anywhere else in the world they want or need to be. Such convenience was unknown just a century ago. When missionaries were called to go to far-off lands, it took them weeks and sometimes months to get close to their ultimate destination. Today, such journeys are generally measured in hours. Literally, everything is accelerating in quantum leaps, and so must we. We need a fresh-from-heaven, rushing, mighty wind. We are entirely too stationary and stagnant. We must, we will, we can by the power of Pentecost reach the unreached at a more rapid pace than ever before. We are positioned and destined to do it. The untold are still untold, but it is not because we can't go to where they are.

Second, there has been an unprecedented explosion in *communication*. This generation has advantages that would have made great science fiction books or movies—sheer fantasy to people even 50 years ago. My uncle made the ultimate sacrifice for America in 1969 at 20 years of age. I've often pondered what it would be like to show him my cell phone. He loved to flip the long spiral cord of his kitchen wall-mounted rotary phone and try to trip me. If I simply tried to explain a few of my phone's features, he would probably think that I'd taken leave of my senses.

A newspaper or a snail mail posted letter 200 years ago would have been that generation's fastest means of receiving news. Beginning in the 19th century and continuing until today, the proliferation of electricity began an information revolution. First, it was the telegraph, then radio, then television. Now, you can hold something in the palm of your hand that can connect with another person, or thousands simultaneously on the other side of the world instantaneously. What used to require months and millions of dollars has now been reduced to seconds and a meager monthly internet bill—and we become impatient when our text message is not answered in five seconds!

Social media, of course, represents another vast category of communication. Due to the lightning-quick progress of technology, a person can record a video wherever they are and get it in front of thousands or even millions of people around the globe in the time it takes to upload it on a website or other media platform. As I stated in my book *Idolatry in America*:

> In fact, we are living in an age of an exponential explosion of knowledge. For example, from Calvary to the time knowledge doubled in the earth was 1,700 years. Between then and the year 1900, knowledge doubled every one hundred years. By 1945, knowledge was doubling every twenty-five years. By 1982, it was doubling roughly every year. By 2020, it was doubling every twelve hours, or quadrupling every day.[15]

Some have called this the information age. It might be better known as the "too much" information age. Nevertheless, a revolution in communication technology has been a boon for preaching, teaching, and sharing the gospel. But if, and only if, we will make use of it to do something of more eternal value than posting pictures and videos of people engaging in mundane, unimpressive, unintellectual, argumentative, petty, silly, crude, rude, embarrassing, self-abasing, self-aggrandizing, gossipy, mean-spirited activity. Seriously, is this what we think Almighty God empowered us with the Holy Ghost of Pentecost and then handed us these tools to do? We don't have to physically move one inch from the sofa to verifiably use our phones or computers to tell the world about the Lord Jesus.

The third area is *finances*. There is more wealth in the world today than at any time in history, and wealth is being created at a bewildering rate. However, an age-old problem remains, which is this: most of the world's wealth is aggregated in the hands of relatively few people. The inevitable result of this is that a few people enjoy benefits that nobody else can dream of, much less achieve, and the masses live quite differently. In fact, millions of people live without even basic necessities, such as clean water and adequate food.

God's purpose is that the gospel should be proclaimed to every person on earth. The Almighty creates wealth and makes wealth available to feed the hungry and clothe the naked. He also provides wealth so that people can finance the preaching of the gospel and the teaching and training of

His people. King Jesus said it like this in the "Our Father" in Matthew 6:9-13:

> *Therefore pray in this manner: Our Father who is in heaven, hallowed be Your name. Your kingdom come; Your will be done on earth as it is in heaven. Give us this day our daily bread. And forgive us our debts, as we forgive our debtors. And lead us not into temptation, but deliver us from evil. For Yours is the kingdom and the power and the glory forever. Amen.*

However, unregenerate people and a lot of Christians tend to be selfish, which means they think of themselves often and others rarely. As a result, they spend huge amounts of money by percentage on things they want, and relatively little to help those less fortunate. Even those known for their philanthropy often fund their own foundations that finance their favorite secular causes, which in many cases have nothing to do with spiritual matters and in no way advance God's kingdom. It is tragic. For these reasons, more money does not automatically translate into more for gospel ministry.

Here is a dilemma: we can get to the lost more efficiently than ever; we can reach them with more means of communication than any previous generation; we have more financial opportunity to help propagate the gospel than at any time in history—and still the great commission remains unfulfilled. I am not criticizing the many organizations that are doing splendid work in missions activity around the world. What I am saying is there is something missing that is keeping our efforts from being as fruitful as we should expect them to be.

This is especially true given all the advantages granted to us by our Father through Jesus Christ and the power of Pentecost to make it happen.

By sheer, raw ferocity of Pentecostal power in the first century, the gospel went from 120 people in Jerusalem to the far reaches of the vast Roman world. It affected life transformation in every place and in every strata of the culture. They had some advantages, to be sure, such as the widespread Roman transportation system and the Greek language, which was common in much of the empire. However, they did not have an entire Bible, printing capacity, mass communication, social media, and the like. Let's face it—they had donkeys, horses, fishing boats and papyrus to write on by candlelight. They did not have automobiles, jet airplanes, ocean liners, and cargo ships. They had no computers equipped with artificial intelligence, no cell phones with voice activation to send messages, no electric lights to extend the daylight into the darkness. Yet they impacted the world with their witness. What was the key to their success?

There is undoubtedly more than one correct answer to that question. However, I believe one significant factor that energized and empowered the first-century church's witness was that many of them—most of them—were filled to overflowing with the Holy Spirit who came on the day of Pentecost! In simple terms, we don't do what they did because we don't have what they had. Until we recognize and remedy our deficiency in this area, our efforts at world evangelization will be about as effective as trying to melt a glacier with a wooden match.

There is a reason we often use the first-century church as a model for that which should be taking place at present. It is not because there were no controversies or differences that needed resolution—there were many. Nor is it that the earliest believers possessed all of the answers or even asked all the right questions. Experience being a master teacher, they learned as they went, just as we do, or as we are obliged to. In the earliest days, the Jewish believers were not even certain that the Gentiles could or would be saved. The paramount reason for our utilization of those first believers as examples is because they represent the most thoroughly scriptural example of what the modern church should reflect.

The fundamental principles they employed should be our template for kingdom achievement and success. A most significant principle was, of course, that they were filled with or baptized with the Holy Spirit. Therefore, they were distinguished by being supernaturally endowed with extraordinary power (1 Corinthians 12:4 AMP) that enabled them to accomplish the divine directive that the Lord Jesus had given them. Namely, this was to go into all the world and preach the gospel to every creature.

The Lord Jesus Christ, the head of the church, has given us this same commission. The orders have not been changed, they have not been abridged or expanded, and neither has the essential equipment available to fulfill them. The modern church cannot, with any degree of expectation, hope to fulfill heaven's assignment unaccompanied by the unparalleled power of the Holy Ghost that both energized and stabilized the original church. The thought that we can fulfill God's plan absent God's Holy Spirit is incomprehensible. Further, it is the ultimate expression of humanism and gross idolatry—the worship of self rather than the living God. It is a sorry spectacle over which the angels hang their heads and weep. Perhaps a refresher course from the ancient book that bears Isaiah's name is appropriate: "For my thoughts are not your thoughts, neither are your ways my ways, saith the Lord" (Isaiah 55:8 KJV). May the Holy Ghost of God shake us back to our spiritual senses.

There's more. When Moses was instructed to build the first earthly house for God, the wilderness tabernacle, Jehovah was specific regarding the involvement of His Spirit.

> *Who serve unto the example and shadow of heavenly things, as Moses was admonished of God when he was about to make the tabernacle: for, See, saith he, that thou make all things according to the pattern shewed to thee in the mount* (Hebrews 8:5 KJV).

How are we aware of modernized churches' neglect or rejection of the Holy Spirit's influence? There are many signs of confirmation.

First among these is that the church's silence is deafening. As exhibited on the day of Pentecost (Acts 2), one of the characteristics of the Holy Spirit's presence is uplifted voices and an increase in volume. Upon this subject I penned a book entitled *Silent No More*. If ever there has been a time in the history of the church of Jesus Christ when our corporate and unified voices must be lifted with a clear and clarion call, it is at this moment, in the midst of a perverse and self-destructive culture. With that deep-throated voice of prophetic declaration we must, with conviction born of prayer, continue to proclaim an eternal message. It was first announced by the Lord Jesus and His disciples, and it is this: "The time is fulfilled, and the kingdom of God is at hand. Repent and believe the gospel" (Mark 1:15).

Of course, such a message is bound to be rejected by generations that have been overly indulged, petted, and pampered by parents, educators, and—certainly not exempt—preachers and pastors. This trend was spawned with the children of Baby Boomers and continues unabated through and continuing beyond Gen Alpha (the first generation fully born in the 21st century). Members of these generations were raised on a steady diet of "you're perfect," "you deserve," "you have a right," "you should be rewarded regardless of effort or participation," and a heaping double portion of "it's not your fault," "there's always someone to blame," and with a beautiful, syrupy sweet dessert of "your self-image is the only thing that matters."

This has all contributed significantly to the preachers of these generations delivering messages and conducting services that are long on inclusion, positivity, and personality and short on the gospel, orthodoxy, and doctrine. In other words, Sunday morning's 45- to 75-minute worship has become little more than a self-help pep rally for spiritual and emotional kindergartners. It requires nothing from the attendees other than, well, attending, but only when it's convenient. It has no resemblance to a Pentecostal encounter with God complete with true worship and an anointed message from

God's Word. These require life change through surrender, repentance, and service to God.

This generation's pastors are no longer men who have been in the mountain with God. These church "front men" much more resemble someone auditioning for a position as a late-night talk-show host, a comedian, or some other entertainer. They should be aspiring to be a firebrand of God, called, anointed, and appointed by Jehovah to proclaim God's Word and lead God's people. This cannot be accomplished by preaching what the people think they want to hear rather than the truth of God that cannot fail to transform human persons.

Righteous parents correct and discipline their children when they do that which is dangerous, immoral, or sinful. They employ God's Word to do so (Romans 12:8). When the pulpit proclaims material outside the word of God and without the precious Holy Spirit to convict men's hearts, no correction is possible. As a result, people cast off all restraint and run wild, doing anything that seems right in their own eyes, leading to cultural chaos (Proverbs 29:18 ESV and NLT). If you're in doubt about this, simply observe it in real time in the disastrous effects in our churches, families, and communities.

The Holy Spirit is also acutely disregarded when churches conceal His presence and mighty works rather than inviting Him through praise, exaltation, and expectancy. What a travesty or blasphemy that even in some Charismatic and Pentecostal worship services, God's Holy Spirit has only a slight, generic mention. Speaking in tongues or other supernatural manifestations are not permitted or tolerated. There is little or no observable distinction between such church gatherings and those that make no claim to believe in the baptism of the Holy Spirit.

There has never been a moment when it has been more immediately imperative for God's church to be distinguished and differentiated from the culture. It should be set apart by its bold and uncompromising stand on the necessity of preaching, teaching, and manifestly living the biblical doctrine of Pentecost in its fullest expression. Our call and purpose is to be different than the secular and pseudo-religious world. We must be willingly joyful in our resolute determination to be easily and manifestly distinguishable from them.

The unregenerate world is not looking for a slightly improved version of the existence they currently have. They are seeking freedom from the pain of hopelessness and the deep, cavernous void in their lives, not for just a temporary respite from it. Their hearts cry out for salvation, deliverance, and healing, and for that total life transformation that only Jesus Christ through the power of the Holy Ghost can give them. They are not searching for something else to busy themselves with or the entanglements of rigorous religious rules. They want and are in need of redemption and the effervescent life force of the Holy Spirit of God alive within them. God has promised it to them and to us, but He will require the Holy Spirit to be involved in such a transformation, causing it to be a right now reality.

The Holy Spirit will not impose Himself or God's will where He is unwelcome or hidden from view. He will refuse to be silenced, slighted, or sealed in a back room or relegated to manifesting only in a small group or home meeting. He must be and will be the very visible, audible fountain flowing forth in our every endeavor of the church and every expression of God's kingdom in our daily lives.

Any church that denies the Holy Spirit's work and influence is a sad and ineffective, timid and intimidated spectacle. It is dead when it should be a resurrected remnant. It retreats when it should be a revenant of revival advancing into enemy-controlled territory. It cowers in fear when its armor reveals that it is built for the battle and created for the conflict. Much of the current churchgoing community can't even be considered as in full-scale retreat—they are being summarily and embarrassingly routed and conquered by hell's forces. They have abandoned the field of battle and now occupy the silent sidelines. They are too weak or uninformed to engage the culture, content to display a weary smile and sniff a few wilted flowers they have picked along the way.

Having separated from the purveyors of Pentecostal power and truth, they are left powerless with no perceived option but to become critical. How heartbreaking. It is eternally jeopardizing and ill-advised to ever speak a word against the Holy Ghost or to attribute any of His divine works to satan.

> *Therefore I say to you, all kinds of sin and blasphemy will be forgiven men, but the blasphemy against the Holy Spirit will not be forgiven men. Whoever speaks a word against the Son of Man will be forgiven. But whoever speaks against the Holy Spirit*

will not be forgiven, neither in this world, nor in the world to come (Matthew 12:31-32).

The Lord Jesus also said in Matthew 25:30, "Throw the unprofitable servant into outer darkness, where there will be weeping and gnashing of teeth." Whatever you do, don't keep drilling holes in the hull of the old ship of Zion and then wonder why we're making no progress!

When the church or a person is without the Spirit of God, they are concealing truth rather than revealing it. The contrasting truths of sin and righteousness blend together in a nebulous shade of gray. Nothing is certain. Nothing is absolute. There is no objective truth—there is only your truth and my truth and their truth. Everyone's personal reality becomes equally as legitimate as anyone else's. The meaning of everything, whether simple or complex, is reduced to opinion or depends on context, nuance, or feelings, or some other parameter that can be neither measured nor defined. God's truth must be manipulated or synthesized, interpreted or contextualized, reimagined or at least rebranded, often rejected or explained away by some other designation.

Here is why: if truth is absolute (and it is), then the truth deniers must acknowledge that they have fallen short of its standard, leaving no options for them other than repentance (Romans 3:23). As a result of pride, they will do anything and everything necessary to avoid that, so they silence their conscience and the Holy Spirit's voice. They work hard to continue to convince themselves and others that something other than the truth is true.

Here is a corollary to the above thought. A church that denies the operation of the Holy Spirit makes things complicated rather than simple. They prefer excessive, extravagant rhetoric rather than plain speech. The reason? If everyone understood it, those in charge would lose their authority. They relish the thought of being the only ones intelligent enough to understand what they are talking about. This aura of intellectual superiority gives them the pretense of power that accompanies their faux expertise on the subject matter.

As you might guess, I have a problem with all that. The Lord Jesus, during His earthly ministry, most often employed everyday, common speech and symbols that the people could readily understand. They might not have *liked* what He said, but there is little question that they *understood* what He said. He didn't couch His discourses in fancy words or in deeply intellectual, philosophical, or theological terminology. Nor should we.

As I have said often, the simplicity of the gospel is its power, and its power is its simplicity. It has been communicated with great power and effect in the following straightforward truths. Jesus loves you. Jesus died for you. Jesus rose from the dead. Jesus can change your life. I know, because He changed mine. A child or someone who has never heard it before can understand, believe, and receive eternal life. The gospel is not a complex puzzle to be solved, but a simple invitation to receive the love of God. Just as a child trusts without hesitation, so must the gospel of Christ be proclaimed and accepted with childlike faith, wide-eyed and openhearted.

But Jesus called the children to him and said, "Let the little children come to me, and do not hinder them, for the kingdom of God belongs to such as these. Truly I tell you, anyone who will not receive the kingdom of God like a little child will never enter it (Luke 18:16-17 NIV).

Any church absent the power of the Holy Spirit will tend to emphasize ritual rather than relationship. Ritual operates under human auspices in acts of formality, liturgy, religious routine, and habit. Rituals, regardless of how meaningful they may be especially at first, void of relationship quickly become dull, dry, and dead. Before long, adherents go through the ritual without even thinking about what they are doing or why they are doing it. Their bodies go through the motions, but ritual loses its power to engage their minds, their emotions, their wills, or their hearts. Dead ritual leads to dead worship.

Relationship, on the other hand, is ever changing and evolving. It is rarely the same from one day or one encounter to the next. Think about the relationships you have with those of your family. Irrespective of the length of time you have known them, the possibility always remains that you will discover something new about them with every new encounter. Simultaneously, they may learn things about you that they had not realized previously, either. Evolving relationships often prove to be exercises in self-realization and discovery, as well. As the result of a continuing relationship, one begins to recognize things about oneself that were previously unknown, or may have been too painful or frightening to admit or to confront.

Relationships can be both comforting and notoriously uncomfortable, which is a prime reason why not a few people avoid them. A continuing vibrant and vital relationship with God the Holy Spirit will certainly result in us discovering new things about Him. This will inevitably require change, adjustment, confession, honesty, and even repentance on our part toward our God. It will also cause each of us to realize things about ourselves that need to change. This is due to the empowering of the Holy Spirit, which enables us to become more like the God we love and serve. In the absence of the Holy Spirit's influence, we will either remain stagnant or drift further and further from the presence and nature and character of our great God.

A church without the influence of the Holy Spirit will emphasize natural things rather than spiritual things. "But the natural man does not receive the things of the Spirit of God, for they are foolishness to him; nor can he know them, because they are spiritually discerned" (1 Corinthians 2:14). You cannot expect a person who was born blind to comprehend the beauty of a sunset in the same way that you do, regardless of how explicitly it might be explained or described. He is not equipped with the capacity to see it with his eyesight as you have been blessed to do. In the same way, you cannot expect natural people to understand spiritual concepts. Those who deny or limit the involvement of the Holy Spirit will have a limited understanding of spiritual things.

Lastly, those churches that choose to deny the power and presence of the Holy Spirit will become inwardly focused rather than outwardly focused. This is the opposite of what the Lord Jesus Christ, the head of the church, commanded us to do. When individuals or organizations become more interested in self than serving others, they begin to die on the inside. When they become obsessed with self, they actually accelerate the process of their own demise. If there is not a seismic shift in their trajectory, they will, like a dying star, implode and fall by their own weight. The Holy Spirit can and will prevent such disastrous collapse if, only if, we will surrender to Him and fully embrace His ministry. In fact, the Holy Spirit of God is on a mission from heaven specifically designed to keep us from falling and destroying ourselves and millions of others. That desired outcome will occur if, only if, we will give Him the priority and the preeminence of which He is deserving and worthy.

Sooner or later, every bill becomes due and payable. The old preacher said it this way, "There's a payday someday!" This is as true for nations as it is for individual consumers. Sadly, at this writing, we are paying for our national rejection of God the Holy Spirit and His ministry through spiritual, moral, and cultural decline, disobedience, and destruction. The only way this abhorrent and loathsome death march can be reversed is with a personal and corporate reckoning. We must here and now recognize our willful rejection of the Holy Spirit, wholeheartedly repent of it, and embrace His glorious, supernatural ministry to us and through us in this pivotal hour of human history. It has happened before. If history is our guide, I believe the conditions are right for it to happen again. If—only if.

CHAPTER SIX

A VERY PRESENT PENTECOST

"The turn of the century." They are but five simple words (seven syllables), but they trigger attention and interest vastly beyond their ordinary pedigree. When I was growing up, having been born in 1957, the phrase indicated the beginning of the 20th century—and it seemed an eternity ago. As an adult, I experienced the turn of the 21st century. I was 13 days short of my 44th birthday. Most folks my age certainly remember the hype and mania associated with the so-called "Y2K" phenomenon. Pundits of all persuasions postulated every system either run or controlled by a computer would be thrown instantly and permanently into complete disarray because of the habit of using only two digits to indicate a year. When the year turned to 00 (the year 2000), every computer would become confused and shut down everything.

I am delighted to report for all the proverbial "Chicken Littles" that the sky did not fall down and the world did not come to an ultimately and cataclysmic end. In fact, with a few slight exceptions, everything went right on as normal, although thousands were left with basements and cellars stacked with canned goods and MREs. I'm sure many of them are still being consumed nearly a quarter century later. This phenomenon points out the heightened expectation that numerous people have concerning the birth of a new century, with all of its potential problems as well as its multitude of possibilities.

America at the beginning of the 20th century was entering an age of just that—endless potential—while dealing with the excesses of the past decades. Several spiritual developments were ongoing, which became forerunners of a movement that would shape the future of the church in America and around the world. They began in relative obscurity, but in a few short years they would gain the attention of nearly every nation on earth.

Topeka, Kansas, may seem like an unlikely place for the seeds of a distinctively Pentecostal movement to have begun, but a seminal moment in Pentecostal history did indeed begin there on New Year's Day 1901. After an all-night prayer meeting, Agnes N. Ozman, a student at Charles F. Parham's Bible school, began speaking in other tongues. There may have been other instances of people speaking in tongues, or praying in the Spirit, before this, but if there were, they went unrecorded. Miss Ozman's experience was very well documented, and it prompted a myriad of others to seek the same

Holy Ghost experience. Soon a small cadre of Pentecostals began to spread their message and testimonies wherever they went. After all, the truest evidence is all about "go ye!"

By 1905, Parham himself moved his efforts to Houston, Texas. Evangelism teams from his school there traveled to numerous cities and communities throughout Texas and elsewhere, spreading the message of Pentecost. Success was elusive at first, and their ministry attracted some adherents while also attracting stern opposition. There were sparks, but something additional was needed in order for the Pentecostal message at the beginning of the 20th century to explode into the worldwide conflagration that it was shortly to become.

These events and those that followed were not without antecedents. I cannot mention the current proliferation of Pentecostal power without also crediting the prior movements that made it possible.

I could go as far back as the Old Testament, as well as including elements of church history that reach back as far as the Protestant Reformation. However, a thorough discussion of that timeline would take a book by itself. My focus here is on how Pentecost spread in the 20th century up to the present moment.

However, as I have said many times, there is much to be gained by a return to the discarded values of the past. Some prior movements and groups deserve mention here because of their profound impact on subsequent events furthering the message of Pentecostal power.

The Moravians were an intrepid band of believers who fled religious persecution while living in Moravia. (In the 20th century, Moravia became a part of Czechoslovakia.) They found respite at the estate of Count Ludwig von Zinzendorf in Saxony, a region of what is now Germany. The small but seriously spiritual group constructed a community there named Herrnhut. In 1727, the town had an unusual visitation of the Holy Spirit in one of their prayer meetings, which revolutionized their fellowship and, in the coming years, the world. God's holy presence fell upon them in an extraordinary way. As a result, the Moravians began to realize that it was the infilling of the Holy Spirit that made an undeniable difference in every situation. There were two foundational pillars of these dynamic Holy Ghost encounters. First was the Moravians' commitment to prayer and, second, their divine zeal to fulfill the great commission by means of missionary activity. In fact, it was Moravian missionaries who impressed a young Anglican minister named John Wesley with their unwavering faith and complete consecration to God and full surrender to the Holy Spirit during a bitterly tempestuous voyage at sea.

John Wesley was inspired by God to develop a strategic and systematic master plan of devotion and service, which became known as a method. He ardently dedicated himself to this method to assist him in his spiritual growth. This same method was readily adopted by Wesley's followers, which is how the name Methodist became popularized. Wesley emphasized with determined devotion the doctrine of holiness, or distilled further, the doctrine of entire sanctification.

He encouraged believers to neither falter nor hesitate in their passionate pursuit of God's presence manifesting in their lives. The founder of the Methodist movement was convinced this could be achieved by dying to self that Christ Jesus by the Holy Spirit could live in and through us.

Those who followed Wesley taught that entire sanctification was a second definite work of divine grace. Some developed this concept even further, and began to teach that a believer who achieved such sanctification could not or would not sin. (Evidence that Wesley himself believed this is quite scant.)

It is worth noting that Wesley had a significant experience related to the Holy Spirit. On May 24, 1738, he attended a Moravian meeting on Aldersgate Street in London. During that gathering, while listening to a reading by Martin Luther's preface to the book of Romans, Wesley felt his heart "strangely warmed." He described this as a profound encounter with God's grace and the assurance of salvation. While it isn't a traditional "baptism in the Holy Spirit" as some Pentecostal or Charismatic groups understand it, this event marked a turning point in Wesley's spiritual journey. His teachings and ministry were deeply influenced by this encounter, emphasizing the transformative work of the Holy Spirit in believers' lives.

Wesley and others who emphasized the doctrine of holiness began to increase rapidly among both clergy and laity, prompting more discussion and promotion of this concept among believers at large. At this time, entire movements were developing holiness unto the Lord as their central theme or message. Organizations and services advancing holiness developed among thousands of Christians who were zealously fervent and continuously hungry for more of God's manifested presence in their lives. There was a growing intensity in the sound to be heard emanating from the tops of the mulberry trees (2 Samuel 5:23-24). Those with ears to hear were sure their God was on the move, and something life-changing, destiny-altering, and history-making had begun. It was raining upstream. The dam was about to break and the flood waters of Pentecost were about to shake the earth. They were correct. Pentecost if—only if.

Parallel to the great holiness movement, increasing numbers of believers began to rediscover and emphasize the biblical doctrine of divine healing. Well-known cases of miraculous healings began to circulate, and healing meetings became quite prevalent. Pentecost if—only if.

As the 20th century approached, the spiritual stage was set. Millions of believers worldwide were interceding for a deeper relationship with their Savior. Ours is a prayer-answering God (Jeremiah 33:3; Matthew 7:7). There came into being a heightened understanding and appreciation of Bible doctrines and orthodoxy that had been neglected for decades. The mundane and ritualistic brand of Christianity fostered by prayerlessness and fed at the table of selfishness was facing its demise. Pentecost would be a renewed emphasis on purity, consecration, and holiness. Services were "off the clock," or click track, making room for the mighty gifts of the Holy Spirit to operate. Included were the gifts of divine healings (1 Corinthians 12:1-11) and deeper dedication to preaching, teaching, and study of God's inerrant Word. Each of these encouraged millions of believers to seek more than the sameness and ordinarily boring and dry church life that was all vast numbers of them had ever experienced. The very idea the God they loved deeply had more in this life for them than they had yet known was beyond exhilarating and incredibly inspiring.

Miss Agnes Ozman's experience of speaking in other tongues in the early morning hours of January 1, 1901, in a Bible school in Topeka was a spark. That spark was about to find the tinder of a people whose hearts had been prepared for more of God than they had ever known. That tiny flame detonated a full-fledged, raging, windswept inferno. It began by igniting one willing and available man sitting in a hallway in Houston, Texas. *Pentecost if.*

William J. Seymour was an African American holiness preacher who had been born to emancipated slaves in Centerville, Louisiana, on May 2, 1870. He had been through many and varied difficulties on his way to that date with divine destiny in the spring of 1906. The preacher had traveled extensively, encountering his share of persecution, privation, and prejudice. A nearly fatal bout of smallpox while he lived in Cincinnati, Ohio, had caused him to lose his left eye. William Seymour supported himself by working as a waiter, a driver, and a porter. He received ordination from the Church of God Reformation—also known as the Evening Light Saints. From there he engaged in itinerant ministry and moved to Houston in 1902. It was there that he met Charles Parham, and they began to work together in outreach efforts. In the early days of 1906, Seymour was attending Parham's school, although he could not by Texas law be in the classroom. As a black man, he was relegated to sitting outside the room in the hall while listening to class lectures. Nevertheless, he persevered.

In February of that year, Seymour accepted an invitation to travel to Los Angeles to preach at a holiness church. After speaking at only one service, he was forthwith disinvited, leaving him with nowhere to preach and nowhere to stay. He found accommodations at Edward Lee's home and began to have gospel meetings at another home in the vicinity. It was during this time that Lee received the baptism of the Holy Spirit and began speaking in tongues.

In short order, like the outbreak of a fever, others began to become infected with the Holy Ghost contagion. By April 12, William Seymour himself received the glorious baptism of the Holy Spirit. *Pentecost if.* The home in which he had been preaching could no longer accommodate the swelling crowds, so the Pentecostal group obtained a building on Azusa Street, which became known as the Apostolic Faith Mission.

Reports and testimonies of demonstrations of Holy Ghost power and presence taking place at Azusa Street could not be confined nor kept silent. The phenomenon spread like the dawn after a dark night throughout the city, and then the nation, and eventually lighting the entire world. For three triumphant, God-exalting, devil-destroying, kingdom-advancing, life-changing, culture-shaking years of Holy Ghost outpouring, daily services were held at the church. Each of them lasted for many hours, from midmorning until as late as midnight. What a contrast to our anemic maximum 75 minute Sunday morning experiences. There were no welcome signs, no jokes, no announcements, no small groups, no light show, no service planning sessions, no follow-up—none of the things that characterize so many modern church services. Although Seymour was undoubtedly the leader, he was often found on the platform with his head hidden in a wooden crate, praying.

To Azusa's Street's detractors, and there were not a few, it all seemed like bedlam. To its adherents seeking the presence and power of their living God, it was verifiably heaven manifested on earth. The difference was, of course, determined by the intention of the visitors. Those who came seeking God encountered Him, despite seeing activity they had never been exposed to or ever imagined would take place in a church. While those who came to mock and make fun of the services were not disappointed, even the most skeptical among them could not deny that something was happening that was far beyond anything ordinary. Within a few brief years, the message of the Pentecostal experience along with speaking in tongues, miracles, healings, gifts, and demonstrations of God's Holy Spirit had spread. It flowed liked waves of the ocean to nearly every city in America and many nations of the world. Pentecost if—only if.

Although the Holy Ghost-filled revival atmosphere at Azusa Street eventually waned, the effects of everything that took place there, and what pilgrims to the revival took with them from there, did nothing but increase exponentially. Within a relatively short span of time, the message of

Pentecost and its unrivaled presence of God Almighty traveled to the corners of the globe. Europe, Russia, Africa, South America, India, and the islands of the sea all saw those who had been filled with the Spirit come to their lands to proclaim the Pentecostal power of God.

Some believed that tongues would give missionaries a supernatural ability to preach the gospel to those of many nations without the preachers learning the respective languages of the people groups to whom they ministered. In this they were much mistaken. While it is true that there have been reported occasions when ministers have spoken in native languages without realizing it, tongues was never intended by God to be a means to communicate on a regular basis with indigenous people. Nevertheless, the Pentecostal revival certainly created a renewed emphasis on missions activity. There it is again: that divine "go ye" mark of Pentecost.

As time went on, distinctly Pentecostal denominations were organized to provide oversight, leadership, and credentialing to Pentecostal ministers. Pentecostal churches continued to spring up in cities and communities the world over unabated.

As the 1920s began, a refreshing, regenerating new wave of revival was released from heaven. It established a renewed emphasis on the doctrines of divine healing and the mighty baptism of the Holy Spirit. Pentecostal ministers circumnavigated the globe, preaching under heavy anointings and ministering with tremendous visitations of miracles, signs, and wonders. Among these were such generals as Aimee Semple McPherson, John G. Lake, Charles S. Price, Raymond T.

Richie, P.C. Nelson, F.F. Bosworth, George and Stephen Jeffreys, Smith Wigglesworth, and a host of others.

This work of the Holy Spirit was attenuated by the Great Depression, which began in 1929 and was unabated for a decade of deprivation. Missions activity continued but was severely hampered by the effects of the depression, which were felt worldwide. On September 1, 1939, immediately following the depression, World War II began in Europe, which drastically restricted travel, especially in areas directly affected by the raging conflict.

However, it was during the years 1934–36 that a miraculous, unlikely, supernatural reunion was forged in the fiery furnace of Pentecost. It began in Eureka Springs, Arkansas. Dr. Howard Carter, then 43 years old, and a young 21-year-old Lester Sumrall embarked on a history-making tour of transformation covering 60,000 miles around the world. They launched from California, spreading flames of Pentecost to mission stations from New Zealand to Stalin's Soviet Union until they finally returned to England.

The Holy Spirit's flaming outpouring had just begun. There were many more chapters yet to be written. At the close of World War II in 1945, another glorious deluge of divine healing and revival, predominantly borne along by Pentecostal men and women, covered the earth from approximately 1947 through 1958. This was the dawning age of tent revivals, conducted by men such as William Branham, Oral Roberts, Jack Coe, A.A. Allen, Tommy Hicks, T.L Osborn, and R.W. Schambach, just to name a few. These Pentecostal pioneers catapulted the message of divine healing and the powerful baptism of the Holy Spirit to uncounted multitudes.

It was during this time that Dr. Lester Sumrall, anointed by and at the direction of the Holy Ghost, exorcised two demons from one possessed Filipino young woman. She was a 17-year-old prostitute named Clarita Villanueva, imprisoned at Bilibid prison in Manila. The revival that resulted from Dr. Sumrall's obedience and the power of the Holy Ghost saw 150,000 adults give their lives to the Lord Jesus Christ in only six weeks' time.

Despite the myriad of signs, wonders, and miracles that transpired during the unprecedented healing revival, the Holy Ghost was still moving mightily in the earth. In the late 1950s and early '60s, millions of ministers and laypeople alike who were faithful members of mainline denominations began to receive the "Acts chapter 2" experience of the baptism of the Holy Spirit. The Holy Ghost wind broke down barriers transcending traditional boundaries, and forthwith speaking in tongues became the language of praise among Presbyterians, Baptists, Lutherans, Episcopalians, Catholics, and numerous others.

Multitudes who had never been exposed to the doctrinal concepts such as the gifts of the Holy Spirit, the manifestation of miracles, and speaking in tongues found themselves immersed in spiritual realities that they had never known were available to them. Believers were energized and awakened, and tens of thousands of churches were turned right side up and transformed. New churches were being planted by those who were rejected or given the left foot of fellowship by those who remained too rigid to accept those now filled with the Holy Ghost. This was categorized as something new when in fact it had been happening since the events of Acts chapter 2! There is truly nothing new under the sun:

> *The thing that hath been, it is that which shall be; and that which is done is that which shall be done: and there is no new thing under the sun* (Ecclesiastes 1:9 KJV).

There was still more to come. The 1970s saw the advent of another group of Pentecostal preachers who preached and taught a return to God's infallible Word as the absolute foundation of every believer's daily life, with a strong emphasis on the doctrine of faith. Faith in God, of course, could not be considered a new concept or doctrine by any means, as it is a foundational aspect of Christianity. Certainly, it has been so since the Reformation's Sola Fida, "faith alone"—man is justified by Christ's finished work, not by personal deeds. However, when the church has lost or is about to lose sight of such a fundamental truth as faith, the Holy Spirit raises up men and women anointed to bring a renewed emphasis to that which has been neglected. Springing forth from earlier ministries such as E.W. Kenyon, A.J. Gordon, George Muller, and Smith Wigglesworth, what became known as the Word of Faith movement began to flow. Kenneth E. Hagin, Kenneth Copeland, Jerry Savelle, Frederick K.C. Price, John Osteen, Charles Capps, Norvel Hayes, and countless others preached and continue to preach faith in God as the bedrock of our Christian lives.

I must mention that with the advent and expansion of multi-network television, as well as cable and satellite television, new Christian networks began to propagate the message of salvation, Pentecost, and the word of faith movement to America and the world. Suddenly there was church and ministry, worship, preaching, and teaching of God's Word available 24/7 to believers and nonbelievers alike.

These developments and many others have contributed to Pentecostals becoming one of the largest groups of Christian believers worldwide—not to mention having the distinction of being the fastest-growing portion of all Christianity. Many of the largest churches in America and the world are Pentecostal, Charismatic, or Full Gospel. The particular designation they have is of slight consequence. What matters is their emphasis upon the presence, power, and utter dependency upon the blessed Holy Spirit in everything they produce for the kingdom of God and of His Christ.

In fact, the largest Christian church on this planet is indeed a Pentecostal church. In 1958, a young man who had recently graduated from Bible school was led by the Holy Spirit to begin a church in a woman's home. A booming crowd of six individuals were in attendance, which included one soaking-wet lady who came in from a nearby bus stop to escape the rain. That small gathering of souls was the seed from which the living God by the power of the Holy Spirit grew what is now the world's largest church—Yoido Full Gospel Church in Seoul, South Korea, founded by Dr. David Yonggi Cho.

I was privileged to visit a Friday evening prayer meeting conducted by this incomprehensible church. As Dr. Lester Sumrall and I walked from our hotel to the service, I could actually feel something vibrating the sidewalk under my feet. As we came closer, I realized it was the reverberation of tens of thousands Holy Spirit-filled believers fervently praying in one voice and in one accord. Yes, I experienced in that moment the unharnessed raw ferocity of Pentecost! I had never witnessed anything like it before or since. They prayed with reckless abandon. They prayed with white-hot zeal. They prayed because they knew their lives, and the lives of those they loved, depended upon their prayers.

It is no longer six God-seeking individuals. The church was said to number 153,000 people, between the mother church and regional chapels, and 830,000 members in 2007. That, my dear friend, is what can happen when the fiery wind of the Holy Ghost encounters the tenderness of hungry hearts. Korea nor the world will remain the same because they are there, praying, worshiping, preaching, serving, witnessing under the divine unction and anointing of Pentecost.

It was my great honor to know Dr. Cho, and I considered him a friend. I am convinced that Spirit-filled believers have and will continue to revolutionize this troubled world. However, that can never be accomplished apart from the absolute reliance upon the direction and divine impartation of the Holy Spirit.

I am not certain exactly how or when the opportunity will be issued from the pavilion of heaven for you and me to participate fully in the next great global move of the Holy

Ghost that will verifiably shake the earth. I am convinced that it is coming. I believe I sense the clouds inundated with the rain of the Holy Ghost. I can faintly see them forming on the horizon over the parched land. Yes, I can now begin to smell the moisture in the arid air. It's Pentecost—if, only if.

In the waiting, we should commit to do something every day, by the Holy Spirit's inspiration, as our personal starting point to change our world—our domain—every place where God Almighty has graced us to have influence. Oh, what unimaginable transformation would take place if in our individual spaces we would take dominion. We would have Pentecost if, only if, we would pray and yield to the moving of the Holy Spirit with great expectation. That can yield the atmosphere that brings the miraculous to birth. We might witness the mighty power of Pentecost released by praying that simple yet profound passage in 1 Chronicles 4:10:

> *And Jabez called on the God of Israel, saying, Oh that thou wouldest bless me indeed, and enlarge my coast, and that thine hand might be with me, and that thou wouldest keep me from evil, that it may not grieve me! And God granted him that which he requested* (KJV).

This is followed only by praying in tongues and anticipating divine activity through the Holy Ghost. Our immediate response to the direction of the Holy Ghost, almost by spiritual reflex in matters that may seem small at the time, will become strategic inflection points and lead us into victories that have world-changing impact. Let me explain what I mean.

It seems to me that perhaps with the Azusa Street revival, and other related divinely orchestrated developments, the living God with outstretched hands was offering His church an unprecedented opportunity. In that particular case, I believe the Holy Ghost was inspiring the church to assume the lead in bringing the generational scourge of racism to an end, along with its repulsive little cousins, sexism and classism.

The Holy Spirit clearly selected William Seymour, a black man, to an elevated position of spiritual leadership to lead the efforts of the Azusa Street church. That resulted in the repercussions of a revival that reverberated around the world. You see, William Seymour was willing to extend his ministry to anyone the Holy Spirit pointed out to him, not only to those who were like him. He did not seek to exclude anyone, regardless of their socioeconomic status, appearance, or even doctrine. As though it were almost a subconscious instinctive reaction, Seymour seemed to recognize that what was taking place was far greater than any single person, group, age, or nationality.

He rightfully had to resist the efforts of some to co-opt the success of the Azusa Street revival for their own selfish ends. However, he had a remarkable ability to forgive wrongs suffered and continue to promote what was happening not for his personal gain, but for the good of the church as a whole. It was the church for which the Lord Jesus Christ had given His life. It was the church for which Jesus was resurrected from the dead and returned to heaven. It was the church to which He sent the Holy Spirit at Pentecost to birth in the earth.

People of all ages, nationalities, races, and religious affiliations came to witness the Pentecostal outpouring at Azusa Street. There were, as always, those who came only to scoff and scorn. However, the vast majority came to behold the great works of God and to encounter the baptism of the Holy Ghost for themselves. I believe that what they saw and involved themselves with was the divine plan of God for His people. At Azusa Street, they were worshiping together without regard to their economic, ethnic, gender, or doctrinal distinctions. As Frank Bartleman famously wrote of those glorious meetings, "The color line was washed away in the blood [of Christ]."

I will remind you that Azusa Street was not the result of any organization offering a seminar, or a marketing group developing an outstanding advertising campaign, or any other type of man-made initiative. The earth-shaking move of Pentecostal power was God sovereignly descending upon His seeking, praying, consecrated people. There simply is no other possibility. Believe me, even greater outpourings are in our individual and corporate future. Pentecost if, only if.

There are other examples of Pentecost crossing the color barrier, as well. I included one in particular in my book *50 Moments of Pentecostal History*:

> Gaston B. Cashwell, a Holiness preacher in the mountains of North Carolina, heard about what was happening at Azusa Street from a magazine article written by Frank Bartleman. He borrowed money to travel to Los Angeles. Although he recognized that the Spirit of God was

moving in the services, he was reluctant to receive prayer from blacks, due to his background of exposure to racism. However, his desire for more of God caused him to repent. He testified that he was delivered of his racial hatred, and Pastor Seymour and other black leaders laid hands on him. He received the baptism of the Holy Spirit and spoke in tongues.[16]

Another representative illustration is that of Charles H. Mason, who in 1897 founded an organization of churches, which he led, designated as the Church of God in Christ (COGIC). He had been preaching for many years, yet still safeguarded a deep desire for more of God's holy presence. I also share his testimonial in *50 Moments of Pentecostal History*:

Mason was still unsatisfied and traveled to Azusa Street in 1906. There, he received the baptism of the Holy Spirit and came home to tell his churches about it. They rejected the message. C.P. Jones went one way, and Mason and those who were receptive to the baptism of the Holy Spirit went another way.

As time went on, many churches under the COGIC banner were white as well as black. Mason sought to have good relationships with leaders of all races, and many white ministers...received credentials under Mason and the COGIC.[17]

A black man was leading an unprecedented revival of Pentecostal power, the effects of which went to the ends of the earth. He did so without racial bias, even while suffering racial hatred, discrimination, and prejudice himself. Another black man led what essentially became the first Pentecostal denomination, and it included both black and white ministers and churches. These promising developments indicate to me that the church had a divine occasion to overturn generations of racial animosity. This we surely know to be the heart of God. John 3:16 says so.

However, as we have seen from subsequent events, the church as a whole was ill-prepared for such a role of leadership. Rather than seizing the moment that was meant to usher in a new era of racial harmony, before very long the awful blight of racism that characterized much of America at that time returned. Deciding not to worship side by side without regard to race, entire groups once again separated themselves by skin color and other distinctions. With few exceptions, leadership roles in many churches were not offered to blacks. They were therefore forced to either settle for whatever accommodations were offered them or required to form their own associations in order to express their God-given giftings and abilities.

The church remained submitted to the culture. Rather than showing the grace needed or the Pentecostal power that was indispensable to dominate the culture, this ill-preparedness of great roles and responsibilities is not an uncommon issue for the church historically. There are many examples that substantiate this uncomfortable truth from modern history.

At the close of World War II in the Pacific, General Douglas MacArthur, the Supreme Commander of Allied Powers, implored Christian organizations to send 10,000 missionaries to Japan, which he described as a "spiritual vacuum."[18] The church as a whole ignored his request. Japan is now less than 2 percent Christian.

United States President Ronald Reagan delivered a speech in West Berlin on June 12, 1987. In it, he famously said in stern tones, "Mr. Gorbachev, tear down this wall!" When the Berlin wall fell in 1989 and communism in the Soviet Union collapsed, in many instances, cult groups arrived in the brand-new mission field before Christians did.

I had the distinct privilege of preaching in the first gospel crusade in Russia in 70 years. The venue was the Lenin Sports Arena in St. Petersburg, the city formerly known as Leningrad. I watched in stunned awe as the hammer and sickle flag of the Soviet Union came down, replaced by the Russian flag. I preached under the anointing of Pentecost as precious persons were instantly liberated from their rickety wheelchairs. I witnessed row after row of Red Army soldiers come streaming from their upper-level seats in the back sections of the 22,000-seat hall to make their way to the altar to receive God's gift of salvation. They were wonderfully born again; many received the baptism of the Holy Ghost and began to speak in tongues and glorify God.

A significant door of utterance had opened to the church, and the nation stood open for a great harvest of souls, prepared for the reaping by the Holy Spirit. While there were a few significant exceptions, the church was sadly not prepared for the opportunity.

Many places in our troubled world have never heard the gospel from an American, but, of course, they have heard about soft drinks and other products made in America.[19]

When someone receives an inspired idea great enough to challenge the current status quo, uninspired modern church, why are they not being celebrated and supported? Far too often they're criticized and told to stop dreaming. How outrageously disheartening. I can think of two examples from the life and ministry of my pastor for many years, Dr. Lester Sumrall.

One idea, which had been given to him by the Holy Spirit, was to preach the gospel by means of shortwave radio to unreached people groups. During his many millions of miles in missionary travels, he was ministering in just such places where people had no contact with the outside world by television or traditional radio. He discovered, however, they did have access to a shortwave radio unit.

Shortwave radio technology differs from other forms of transmission because the radio waves are not line of sight, as with FM (frequency modulated) radio waves. AM (amplitude modulated) radio waves can be heard for much longer distances, but in the daytime, especially, they are limited by interference from other electromagnetic impulses. At night, they can be heard for longer distances. In shortwave transmission, the radio waves are reflected off the ionosphere day or night, causing the messages carried by them to travel unabated all over the world.

Dr. Sumrall's efforts to receive a license to develop a shortwave transmitter was thwarted for years by the federal government. Finally, upon receiving his long-awaited approval, he joyfully began to broadcast the gospel of Jesus Christ around the literal globe from one location. His Holy Ghost-inspired idea was ahead of its time. I was gratified to be with him to "throw the switch" and see the miracle begin.

Additionally, Dr. Sumrall had received a divine visitation from the Lord in Jerusalem, Israel, which began with these prophetic words, "It's midnight prophetically. I am concerned that My people will starve to death before I come." Then the Lord directed him to write the entire plan for the End Time Joseph Feed the Hungry initiative. (I was privileged to be there with him the day he received this vision from the Holy Spirit.) This program has resulted in food relief being available to many millions of people in areas hit by the dark specter of famine. His ministry purchased a C-130 Hercules cargo aircraft and an ocean-going ship to transport food and medical supplies to places where it is most desperately needed. Again, I was honored to participate in both of their dedication ceremonies into the kingdom of God.

These are but two examples of the kind of forward-thinking, big-picture ideas that the church must continue to receive in order to effectively proclaim the gospel of Christ around the world with Pentecostal power. If, only if. These heavenly visions of the Holy Ghost were not the result of a brainstorming session over pizza or a corporate-branding session. They were deposited spiritually just as the Holy Spirit after Pentecost instructed Barnabas and Saul to begin their first missionary journey. Please read Acts 13 and 14 and realize how the Holy Ghost wants to be intimately involved in our lives.

There is no doubt that God is intricately interested in us as individuals, but may we ever be mindful that our great God is just as interested in every other member of the human family. I'm desperately thankful that King Jesus died for me, but how rich is the revelation that He died for much more than me! He gave His life on that rugged rail so that everyone on earth could know Him in the full pardon and the forgiveness of their sins. Through the baptism of the Holy Spirit, we must be ready for and anticipating every kingdom opportunity.

> *But if the Spirit of Him who raised Jesus from the dead lives in you, He who raised Christ from the dead will also give life to your mortal bodies through His Spirit that lives in you* (Romans 8:11).

We must embrace the mighty ministry of the Holy Spirit. It is He alone who is able to position us, prepare us, and empower us with supernatural direction to take complete advantage of every moment of kingdom advancement He affords to us. He is working His plan, even now, for us to present the living hope of the gospel to a dying world with signs, wonders, and miracles following the proclamation of His word in us, living and moving in our mortal bodies.

CHAPTER SEVEN

PENTECOSTAL REVIVAL IF—ONLY IF

Many years ago, my parents built a ranch-style home not far from where our first church building would eventually be constructed. That home was where I lived when I graduated from high school, back around the Bronze Age—1975. Shortly after, I attended Bible college and launched our fledgling church when I was a sophomore. I am still pastoring that same church today. My father had always built our homes, and he was partial to wooded lots. This home's lot was particularly attractive. It boasted several majestic American beech trees. They were tall and graceful and provided welcome shade in the summer and abundant nuts for birds, squirrels, and other animals in the fall.

One year a strong summer thunderstorm with excessive winds and heavy lightning passed through and split one of the mighty hardwoods in the front yard in half. The top half was sent crashing through our home, essentially breaking it in half, as well. No one was injured because it was Sunday evening and we were all in a church service! Nonetheless, it was a devastating event for our family. The cleanup and repair efforts demanded months, requiring us to live in a hotel until the home was livable again. As we examined the tree, we discovered that although it appeared strong and stately on the outside, at the core it was rotted out and hollow. It seemed magnificent, standing tall as long as there were no additional stresses, but when the adverse winds blew and the lightning struck, the strain became too much for it to withstand, and it met its demise.

Something very similar happens to nations. They may appear strong and prosperous by every measurable economic metric, but when they become rotten inside, any increased stress can place them in peril. When a nation eventually fails, that collapse is not merely incidental; it is, in a word, spectacular, causing incalculable damage.

Without getting into the weeds of a technical discussion of the second law of thermodynamics, I suggest that entropy is a classic feature of every era, civilization, people group, or culture. Entropy, as I am using the term here, describes a gradual decline into disorder. If I were preaching, I'd definitely repeat that, so indulge me please—"a gradual decline into disorder." Without some outside force or influence that changes it, every culture will continue to diminish until it is either overthrown from without or hollowed out from within. Either outcome results in a culture becoming irreversibly changed, so much that it becomes indistinguishable—it ceases to exist. This has been the recurring theme throughout human history.

Abraham Lincoln became aware of this dynamic as a young man and identified what he saw as the major threat to America. He said in his speech, "The Perpetuation of our Political Institutions" on January 27, 1838, "If destruction be our lot, we must ourselves be its author and finisher. As a nation of freemen, we must live through all time, or die by suicide."[20] What Lincoln was addressing was that the genuine threat to any culture and its institutions would not be advanced from other nations as much as it would be activated from within its own citizenry. Lincoln presciently warned against an erosion of respect for the laws, customs, and moral imperatives that upheld and sustained any culture.

I am helplessly addicted to plain speech, and I am compelled to engage in it here. Our nation is not solely rotten at the core; it is hollow at the core. The howling winds of adversarial transformation are blowing, perhaps more profoundly and powerfully than at any time in our nation's history—certainly with greater force than at any point in my lifetime. Without an external influence strong enough to overcome the entropy and inertia that threatens to overtake us, we are well on our way to a catastrophic, cataclysmic, comprehensive cultural collapse. Pentecost if—only if!

That conclusion is certainly not a news flash to many. Take heart! Here's the rest of the story. The only true and living Creator God has already masterfully prepared just such an external force that is beyond capable to reverse the disastrous and deadly direction of our nation and the world. The external force of which I write is the unparalleled influence of the Holy Spirit.

We must fully reject powerless, grandiose words of preachers. Chares H. Spurgeon agreed: "Let eloquence be flung to the dogs, rather than souls be lost. We want to win souls, and they are not to be won by flowery speeches."[21] What we require is the presence, the purpose, and the power of the Holy Spirit returned to our institutions, our communities and churches, to our families, and our individual lives. The apostle Paul, undoubtedly a persuasive preacher, said as much in 1 Corinthians 2:4-5:

> *My speech and my preaching was not with enticing words of man's wisdom, but in demonstration of the Spirit and of power, so that your faith should not stand in the wisdom of men, but in the power of God.*

A crisis of the magnitude we now face demands the Holy Spirit's direct *involvement*—more so, it demands His divine *intervention*. With Him, our future is bright. Without Him, our future is beyond grim.

It is important to understand that although we serve a sovereign God, He is in no way dictatorial. In contrast, He so values freedom that He has voluntarily limited His right to intervene in the affairs of men. God so respects free moral agency that He created us with it as standard equipment. When our pristine parents surrendered it in Eden at a tree,

King Jesus purchased back for us in a garden called Gethse-mane. By His sacrificial surrender on Calvary's rugged rail, He will wait to be asked to move in our lives, in our nation, and in our world. The eternal Word of God makes it clear. When Rebekah was pregnant with twins, she inquired of the Lord about her unusual pregnancy. The Lord revealed that two nations were in her womb (Genesis 25:22-23). King David frequently inquired of the Lord before making deci-sions. At one point he asked if he should go up against the Philistines and God assured him of victory (2 Samuel 5:19). In Ezekiel, the Lord God strongly states that He will yet be inquired of by the house of Israel. He multiplied them like a flock (Ezekiel 36:37). What, then, is the answer to this dilemma?

It is simply this: individual believers, church congrega-tions, and pastors (as well as other ministry gift offices) must ask for, indeed plead for, and then allow the blessed Holy Spirit to have priority and ascendancy in their messages, their assemblies, and in their lives. This is a matter of dire neces-sity, and it is crucial for cultural survival. We must never find ourselves guilty, as so many are, of relegating the Holy Spir-it's operation to a back room or to some secondary status. We must now, tomorrow, and forever allow Him to move, to manifest Himself, and most importantly, to motivate multi-tudes to receive radical, revenant, redemptive change. I expect that this is what it will look like, so that we will not be taken by surprise when (not *if*, but *when*) it happens. Pentecost if—only if!

I will begin with no less an authority than the Lord Jesus Christ. His words were crystal clear and He did not hesitate to speak them. Here they are, as recorded in Mark 16:15-18:

> *Go into all the world, and preach the gospel to every creature. He who believes and is baptized will be saved. But he who does not believe will be condemned. These signs will accompany those who believe: In My name they will cast out demons; they will speak with new tongues; they will take up serpents; if they drink any deadly thing, it will not hurt them; they will lay hands on the sick, and they will recover.*

The Lord Jesus was direct and spoke with detailed precision—sign-gift ministry would inevitably accompany the true preaching of the gospel. The inaugural sign that He announced would result in ruffling a great number of religious feathers—believers would cast out demons in His name. Those who would maintain that the devil and his diabolical underlings are not real are making a vain attempt to refute a New Testament doctrinal truth that was directed and affirmed by the resurrected King of glory Himself.

I have offered this recommendation to churchgoers for many years: if you attend a church where they do not believe in casting out demons, don't walk from such a place, but run full stride and never look back. You must not place yourself and your family at such perilous risk. You have no idea what other biblical orthodoxy has been erased from holy writ by those who do not believe and practice such a divine directive as this. Your spiritual life and growth are too valuable to trifle with.

The next sign King Jesus declared would accompany believers is nearly as controversial as the first one—they shall speak with new tongues. This is undoubtedly referring to an initial physical evidence of the baptism of the Holy Spirit, that of supernaturally speaking in an unknown tongue—which is to say, a language that is unknown to the speaker. I will have more to say about this shortly.

I will deal with the next two orders given by our Commander in Chief and Head of the Church together: "they shall take up serpents; and if they drink any deadly thing, it will not hurt them." Jesus was in no way ordering or even recommending that New Testament believers should physically handle snakes or drink poison as a test of their faith. To hold that the Master was so mandating seems an almost obtuse misrepresentation and misinterpretation of His words.

The instruction involving snakes had two meanings. One is that if you accidently became the victim of a poisonous snakebite, and there were no alternatives, you could trust God to protect you, as Paul the apostle did (see Acts 28:3-6). I would not recommend Paul's course of action unless you are walking in Paul's level of faith. Another meaning is as Jesus described the power available to New Testament believers in Luke 10:19: "Look, I give you authority to trample on serpents and scorpions, and over all the power of the enemy. And nothing shall by any means hurt you." Serpents and scorpions are representative of the power of the evil one, and the risen Christ assured us in no uncertain terms that we have total dominion and absolute authority over them all. Regarding drinking deadly things, it is unmistakably stated using the clarifying monosyllable "if," indicating an accidental or inadvertent and not intentional ingestion.

The concluding sign gift given has also captured substantial attention over the past few decades: "they will lay hands on the sick, and they will recover." Few doctrines are as comprehensively confirmed while being as seriously opposed as physical healing as part of the redemptive work of Christ. A thorough treatment of the subject would fill many volumes in itself. Let it suffice to say that Jehovah Rapha, the self-existent God who heals, desires for His people to be healthy in their physical bodies just as surely as He wants them to be well in their souls and spirits.

A very common objection to divine healing would be along these lines: "If God wants people to be well, why isn't everyone well?" The most direct answer would be that if that logic applies then why don't we question likewise, "If God wants all people to be saved (and He does), why isn't everyone saved?" Faith is involved in both of these questions and in their answers. Faith in God is required to be saved (born again), and it is also required to receive physical healing.

I have often referred to the baptism of the Holy Ghost as the gateway to the gifts of the Spirit. While it is possible that believers may receive and operate in one or more of the spiritual gifts without receiving the baptism of the Holy Spirit, it is rare. Allow me to clarify my meaning by using the phrase the "gifts of the Spirit," since there are three separate and distinct lists of such gifts in the New Testament. The first and most commonly preached and taught about and therefore understood is recorded in 1 Corinthians 12:8-10. I refer to these as the *manifestation* gifts of the Holy Spirit. Another list appears in Romans 12:6-8. These are what I refer to as the *motivational* gifts of the Holy Spirit—this list is frequently overlooked entirely. The third listing is found in Ephesians 4:11, and these are referenced as the fivefold *ministry* office gifts.

My purpose here is to focus on the nine manifestation gifts of the Holy Spirit chronicled in 1 Corinthians 12. They are comprised of nine gifts that can be easily divided into three distinct categories. This arrangement was revealed by God's Spirit to Dr. Howard Carter, a British Bible teacher who became a mentor and friend to Dr. Lester Sumrall in the 1930s and thereafter. Dr. Carter was serving a prison sentence as a conscientious objector during World War I. While there, he was studying and meditating on the Word of God. The inspiration of the Holy Ghost filled that place with presence and his seeking heart with revelation knowledge and supernatural insight. Dr. Carter's understanding of the manifestation gifts of the Spirit became and remains the gold standard in Pentecostal theology to this day.

There are three *revelation* gifts:

- The word of wisdom—supernatural insight into the purpose of God, having to do with the future

- The word of knowledge—supernatural information regarding people, places, and things that would otherwise be unknown and unknowable, and having to do with the present rather than the future

- The discerning of spirits—supernatural ability to sense the presence and identity of spirits, whether demonic, angelic, or human spirits

There are three *power* gifts:

- The gift of faith—supernatural ability to trust God, especially in times of difficulty or danger
- The gift of the working of miracles—supernatural ability to control, suspend, or alter natural forces
- The gifts of healings—supernatural ability to heal physical, emotional, or spiritual maladies or malfunctions

There are three *vocal* gifts:

- Prophecy—speaking a supernatural message of exhortation, edification, and comfort in a known language
- Diverse kinds of tongues—supernaturally speaking a message in a language not known to the speaker (it may or may not be known to the hearer or hearers)
- The interpretation of tongues—supernatural ability to show the meaning of a message

in tongues (an interpretation, not a word for
word translation)

Please note that each of these gifts are totally and completely supernatural manifestations of the Holy Spirit. They
have nothing at all to do with a person's education or level of
intellectual capability. I am staunchly in favor of education,
and I encourage everyone to gain as much knowledge as possible to aid and enable them in the pursuit of God's purpose
for their lives. However, the operations of the manifestation
gifts of the Holy Spirit are for everyone, regardless of their
academic experience or ability.

As the glorious, God-breathed charismatic revival progressed through the 1960s and into the 1970s, tens of thousands of individuals from traditional denominational church
backgrounds came into contact with and subsequently
received the mighty baptism of the Holy Spirit. Accompanying their experiences also came access to the manifestation
gifts of the Spirit. As you might guess, this created a tumultuous stir among a number of established organizations as
well as individual churches. Some of the churches adopted
a moderate approach to these developments, while others
forcefully forbade such occurrences in no uncertain terms.

A well-known mainline denominational pastor shared
this story with me. He decided he was going to decisively
and permanently end the controversy raging about the gifts
of the Holy Spirit for his local church. He developed a message upon the premise that all the gifts of the Spirit had been
expeditiously rendered outmoded and irrelevant by modern
developments unknown in previous ages. According to him,

and in keeping with his denomination's doctrinal position on the matter, the gifts of healing were nothing more than the advancements of modern medicine. Tongues was explained as the increased linguistic ability of those who had learned several languages in university studies. The word of knowledge was defined as the vast potential for learning available from advanced educational degree programs. I'm sure by now you are getting the picture.

He continued on this path for some time, but he then began to notice that the longer he spoke, the more conflicted and confused he became. Finally, in a moment of unprecedented perplexity (not to mention absolute honesty), he abruptly ended his sermon with this disclaimer: "Ladies and gentlemen, I have no earthly idea what I am talking about!" He promptly walked off the platform while one of his bewildered associates brought the service to a chaotic conclusion.

Sometime afterward, the pastor himself received the powerful baptism of the Holy Spirit and became a prominent preacher of the Pentecostal persuasion. Pentecost if—only if!

Make no mistake—when men and women in earnest seek and receive the baptism of the Holy Spirit, all of the gifts of the Spirit become available to become operative in their lives. Let me use the revelation gifts of the Spirit as an example. Be assured our great God does not reveal things to individuals about others in order to satisfy their inordinate curiosity or aggrandize their persona. The purposes of the Holy Ghost are always redemptive in nature. Those of you who have teenagers, or remember when you did, may identify with this scenario or a similar one.

Your teen comes home later than usual. You, as a conscientious parent, question them about their whereabouts and their activities. They make an attempt to respond by subscribing to the theory that the truth is like a ladder—it won't support you if it isn't slanted. What they do not realize is that the Holy Spirit of God has already revealed to you, by the gift of the word of knowledge, where they actually were. The Holy Spirit also told you about the extracurricular pursuits wherein they had involved themselves prior to their late arrival at home. You can see how this outcome would give tremendous trepidation to any of your precious teenagers who are tempted in the future to circumvent your requirements for correct behavior when you are not with them. It would give pause to satan as well to know that you were in possession of inside information from the living God Himself.

Perhaps the greatest source of controversy involving the manifestation gifts of the Spirit is the use of the vocal gifts—that is, tongues, interpretation of tongues, and prophecy—in public assemblies, meaning church services in most cases. The purpose of vocal gifts is to "say something." This also caused questions during the infancy of Christ's church in the first century, and Paul dealt with it in specificity by giving guidelines to the church at Corinth in 1 Corinthians chapter 12, and to a larger degree in chapter 14. In these passages, the apostle sets some commonsense parameters to govern the use of vocal gifts to prevent confusion while increasing edification. I recommend that everyone who has been a recipient of the baptism of the Holy Spirit review and become familiar with this wisdom and guidance.

The power gifts are those gifts that "do something." The gift of faith is not distinctly separate from that faith which is given to everyone in a measure when they are born again (Romans 12:3). This type of faith—or as some translations render it, the gift of *special* faith—enables the recipient to realize a miracle that would otherwise be beyond their ordinary faith's ability to produce.

In much the same way, the gift of the working of miracles extends far beyond the ordinary. Remember, all the gifts of the Holy Ghost are supernaturally endowed. These mighty manifestations are in no way of human origin. Often the gift of working of miracles will involve a creative miracle, such as raising the dead or other such displays of God's creative capacity and power.

The gifts of healings are the only one of the nine manifestation gifts that is plural (1 Corinthians 12:28). The subject has never been lacking in depth or breadth of discussion especially regarding the reason for this, and varying theories have been put forward, which have produced no consensus. I don't recommend spending time debating the issue. I am satisfied to accept this truth at face value and simply be thankful that our great God has made these glorious gifts available to us through the Holy Ghost.

A word here on the issue of speaking in tongues. There has been quite a bit of controversy in the church about the significance of speaking in tongues, beginning with its purpose. Many Pentecostals have maintained that speaking in tongues is the (only) evidence of being baptized with the Holy Spirit. One of the problems that arises with this determination is in over-emphasizing speaking in tongues to the diminishing of other important aspects of being baptized with the Holy Spirit.

Another common misconception is that being baptized with the Holy Spirit is a sign of increased spirituality or growth. It is nothing of the sort. The baptism of the Holy Spirit cannot be earned or deserved by good behavior, spiritual exercise, or a commitment to holiness. I am not implying that any of those things are negative for the believer. What I am stating is that the baptism of the Holy Spirit is not granted as an award for meeting some unrealistic religious standard. It is, without any room for debate, a gift! It must be received completely by faith and faith alone, just as is the case with anything else we receive from God. The single requirement for receiving the baptism of the Holy Spirit is that you must be born again. It is in no way connected to one's spiritual maturity.

As to the main purpose for the baptism of the Holy Spirit, that is clearly defined in Acts 1:8: "But you shall receive power when the Holy Spirit comes upon you. And you shall be My witnesses in Jerusalem, and in all Judea and Samaria, and to the ends of the earth." It is quite evident that the motivation of God in filling believers to overflowing with His Spirit is to supernaturally enable them to be witnesses heralding His gospel and grace, goodness, and glory. That becomes our purpose. The gift of the baptism in the Holy Spirit will not supernaturally change you instantly into a spiritually mature believer; that is a product of daily spiritual discipline—especially attending to the disciplines of church attendance

(Hebrews 10:25), Bible reading and study (2 Timothy 2:15), and prayer (1 Thessalonians 5:17).

The ability to speak in tongues accompanies being baptized with the Holy Spirit. It conveys no automatic, special privilege, nor does it indicate any level of advanced spirituality. Speaking in tongues is no indication whatsoever that a person has developed more of the character of God in their lives. In fact, there are those believers who speak in tongues with astounding fluency, yet little of the character of Christ is evidenced by their behavior. There are those who remain just as mean and jealous, just as unforgiving and gossipy as they were before they were filled with the Spirit. In the words of James: "Out of the same mouth proceed blessing and cursing. My brothers, these things ought not to be so" (James 3:10). It is unfortunate that such confused individuals use speaking in tongues as evidence that they have somehow arrived spiritually, whatever they intend that to mean.

I would agree that speaking in tongues is the initial *physical* evidence of the baptism with the Holy Spirit. However, there should be caution in attempting to elevate it as an end in itself to the neglect of such other indicators of the Spirit's work such as a love for others, a passion, if not compulsion, to win lost souls, and an unquenchable determination to submit to God's absolute authority in all matters large and small. I have no doubt we should receive every gift God is pleased to give us, but in all our getting we must continue to develop the fruit of the Spirit, which is the character of God, in our lives as well.

Let me address another issue—it is this: there are those who say they have received the baptism of the Holy Spirit, but they do not speak in tongues, nor do they possess any desire to do so. There are five specific instances for our instruction in this matter recorded in the book of Acts where people receive the baptism with the Holy Spirit. (See Acts 2, 8, 9, 10, and 19.) In three of these instances (Acts 2, 10, and 19), we see individuals who are witnessed to begin to speak in tongues immediately. In the other two instances (Acts 8 and 9), although speaking in tongues is not specifically mentioned, it is implied from the context of the passage. Those who claim to be Spirit filled but do not speak in tongues are certainly the exception, not the rule. In addition, why would anyone refuse something that God offers as a supernatural gift, freely given to His people? It would seem odd for any believer to claim that what God makes available to Christians would ever be considered to be of no value or unnecessary.

Here are three fundamental benefits of speaking in tongues. (Allow me the latitude to mention here that speaking in tongues and praying in the Spirit are essentially equivalent terms, according to 1 Corinthians 14:13-15.)

- First, it is a supernatural means of communication with God, your heavenly Father: "For he who speaks in an unknown tongue does not speak to men, but to God" (1 Corinthians 14:2).

- Second, it enables you to pray the divine will of God in every situation and circumstance: "Likewise, the Spirit helps us in our weaknesses, for we do not know what to pray for as we ought, but the Spirit Himself intercedes for us with groanings too deep for words. He who searches the hearts knows what the mind of the Spirit is, because He intercedes for the saints according to the will of God" (Romans 8:26-27).

- Third, it enables you to build yourself up spiritually: "But you, beloved, build your-selves up in your most holy faith. Pray in the Holy Spirit" (Jude 20).

For those who may have questions concerning how to receive the baptism of the Holy Spirit, I believe you will find this excerpt from my book on that subject helpful, entitled *The Fire Within: A Guide to the Baptism of the Holy Spirit*:

God did not save us just so we could attend re-ligious services while waiting to make the trip to glory. We have been enlisted in an army of saints who are contending for the faith and tak-ing enemy held territory.

Christianity is not and has never been about us—it is about the multitudes that are still in darkness, and it is up to us to shine the light of truth into their lives. In order to do that effec-tively, the baptism of the Holy Spirit is not an option, it is a necessity.

Being filled with the Holy Spirit is not as com-plicated as some have made it seem. I have heard of some groups saying that people have to tarry—or wait—for an unspecified amount of time before they can receive. Others say that candidates must achieve certain requirements of spiritual growth or maturity in order to be eligible to receive the fullness of the Holy Spirit. I don't see any of those restrictions in the Bible.

In fact, in the case of Cornelius in Acts 10, the entire group was saved and instantaneously filled with the Holy Spirit in the same event. It was a surprise to Peter and a shock to his Jewish companions. The recipients didn't even ask for it, although no doubt their hearts were prepared to receive whatever God had for them.

The Holy Spirit just came upon them as they heard the word of God being proclaimed, without any formal request or procedure whatsoever. What this says to me is that God wants people to have this experience more than they want to receive it.

Let me share with you some principles that I have found useful in ministering to people who desire to receive the baptism of the Holy Spirit.

Keep in mind that all baptisms, regardless of what kind they are, have three things in common: the candidate, the element, and the baptizer. In the case of water baptism, the candidate is the believer, the element is the water, and the baptizer is the minister or other person who is actually doing the baptizing.

When it comes to the baptism of the Holy Spirit, the candidate is the believer who wants to receive, the element is the Holy Spirit Himself, and the baptizer is the Lord Jesus Christ.

The only prerequisite for receiving is that a person be born again. If they are not, I lead them in a prayer of salvation. They have just confirmed their eligibility. In fact, you may find, as I have, that new believers are among those who receive the baptism of the Holy Spirit the most readily. Often, they are willing and eager to get all God has for them.

Make sure that those to whom you minister actually understand what they are expecting. If you are not sure, ask them to articulate what they want. If they are uncertain, a few words of explanation are in order.

Let me mention this also—children can and do receive the baptism of the Holy Spirit. I won't presume to tell parents when this should happen in their child's life, but one indicator that they are ready to receive is when they begin to ask questions about the Holy Spirit. I have seen many children receive the baptism of the Holy Spirit—sometimes an entire group of them at once.

Here is a passage that is helpful to increase people's confidence as they prepare to ask for the baptism of the Holy Spirit. Jesus said in Luke 11:9-13:

And I tell you, ask, and it will be given to you; seek, and you will find; knock, and it will be opened to you. For everyone who asks receives, and he who seeks finds, and to him who knocks it will be opened.

If a son asks for bread from any of you who is a father, will you give him a stone? Or if he asks for a fish, will you give him a serpent instead of a fish? Or if he asks for an egg, will you offer him a scorpion? If you then, being evil, know how to give good gifts to your children, how much more will your heavenly Father give the Holy Spirit to those who ask Him?

All anyone who is born again needs to do to receive the baptism of the Holy Spirit is to ask. God will grant their request. Here is a simple prayer that you can lead people to pray as they receive.

Heavenly Father, You said that if I would ask, You would give me the baptism of the Holy Spirit. So right now, I ask You to fill me to overflowing with Your Spirit. I expect to receive power to be a witness. I expect to speak with other tongues as the Spirit gives me the words to say. I am asking in the name of Jesus. Amen.

After this prayer is concluded, I find it helpful to begin thanking God aloud, and I encourage them to do the same. Then, at some point soon after this, I recommend that you begin praying in the Spirit, and encourage them to do the same. Many times they will begin without hesitation.

If they do not, it is important for you to assure them that they have received exactly what they requested, even though they may not have begun speaking in tongues immediately. Remind them of Luke 11:13, where Jesus said their heavenly Father would give the Holy Spirit to those who ask Him for it.[22]

We are partakers of every blessing of God by faith. The proof that they have received is what God's Word says, not whether they immediately begin to speak in tongues. They are assured they can anticipate the manifestation of speaking in that heavenly language!

> *"Believe in me so that rivers of living water will burst out from within you, flowing from your inner-most being, just like the Scripture says!"*
>
> *Jesus was prophesying about the Holy Spirit that believers were being prepared to receive. But the Holy Spirit had not yet been poured out upon them, because Jesus had not yet been unveiled in his full splendor* (John 7:38-39 TPT).

I believe that in the days to come, individuals, as well as those churches that are distinctively Pentecostal, will become even more vital as we anticipate the culture-shaking revival that God will surely send to this blue marble planet before the return of our soon coming King.

Those of us who were forged in the fiery wind of Pentecost could never fear it nor resist it. Rather, we plead fervently for its divine dispersion. Pentecost if—only if! Where are those among us who will grasp hold of the horns of the altar, waiting, seeking, until an inferno sweeps through our hearts, homes, churches, and nations? Pentecost if—only if! That resounding call of Christ has its genesis, as it does for revival, with that single monosyllable, "if."

> *If my people, who are called by my name, will humble themselves and pray and seek my face and turn from their wicked ways, then I will hear from heaven, and I will forgive their sin and will heal their land* (2 Chronicles 7:14 NIV).

If—then. Every blessing afforded to us as believers is without question conditional. The Almighty promises "this" when we first respond to His "that." He will do "this" when we do "that." If my people—*if!* Then I (God) will respond because the condition has been met.

I take liberty here to lift a few powerful and pertinent lines from the prequel of this work, *Revival If…Igniting Your Passion for Personal Renewal and National Revival*:

> God has not changed! The writer of Hebrews shouted it: "Jesus Christ is the same yesterday,

and today, and forever" (13:8). The problem is
not with the living God; the problem is, as always, with us. The problem is the church. We
need to be revived! We need to humble ourselves
before God and pray to our Father, who answers
by fire. We must wholeheartedly seek the face
of the Lord Jesus and turn completely, entirely
from our sins of omission and commission.[23]

There was a noted a pattern in the revivals of history:

> In every case, the revival began with a sin-
> gle individual. A single revived individual.
> Nation-shaking, culture-transforming, histo-
> ry-making revivals begin with one individual in
> personal revival. So I must ask you:
> Could you be that "one"? Are you willing? Are
> you prepared to experience the refreshing, reve-
> nant rain of personal revival? If... Only if![24]

Today America is in the death grip of a severe drought of
Pentecostal power. Our nation withers and shrivels, having
fully embraced secularism, humanism, postmodern relativ-
ism, sexual hedonism, and a pantheon of idols. The rain we
are in desperate need of has a name that strikes modern ears
as hopelessly old-fashioned and outlandishly outdated. It's
called Pentecostal revival.

Where are the people and prophets of God who will weep
between the porch and the altar, calling us back to the discarded values of the past, blowing the trumpet in Zion, sanc-
tifying a fast and calling a solemn assembly?

Where are the Holy Ghost vessels of God intoxicated by the Holy Spirit's intercession flowing forth from sanctified hearts bombarding heaven in our altars? In fact, where are our altars? That is, after all, the place where Jehovah God comes to consume our sacrifices. Where are those paralyzed in travail crying out to their holy God with groanings and unintelligible utterances, with tongues like as of fire sitting upon them? Only they can turn the tide. Where are those possessed with passion for lost and dying, hell-bound souls? Who, like Beniah, will walk into a pit on a snowy day and slay the lions of false doctrine with their industrial complex of entertainment Christianity? God give us those prophets, not profiteers, Holy Ghost preachers of the gospel, not hungover manipulators of men leading the unthinking, undiscerning masses into the perpetration of their own perversions.

We must repent. And we are obliged to turn back to the old ways. This is the divine directive of heaven—to raise up a culturally incorrect army of redemptive change before we're forever doomed to unfruitfulness and the world is forever lost!

Matthew 24:14 (KJV) states, "*This* gospel of the king-dom shall be preached in all the world for a witness unto all nations; and then shall the end come." *This* gospel—not another. The apex of all Christian endeavor must become to place the jewel of a soul in the crown of our Savior that the Lamb of God slain may receive the reward of His suffering. The simplicity of the gospel is its power, and its power is its simplicity. Here it is:

1. Jesus loves you. Brennan Manning has said, "Your Christian life and mine make no

sense unless in the depth of our being we believe that Jesus loves us as we are, not as we should be, because we're never going to be as we should be. Do you really believe that Jesus Christ loves you, not the person next to you, the church, the world—but that He loves you beyond worthiness and un-worthiness, beyond fidelity and infidelity, when you get it right and when you get it wrong? God loves you in the morning sun and the evening rain, without caution or re-gret, without boundary or limit, no matter what's gone down, God simply can't stop loving you" (John 3:16).[25]

2. Jesus died for you (John 15:13).

3. Jesus rose from the dead (Matthew 28:1-6).

4. Jesus can change your life (2 Corinthians 5:17). (I know He can, because He changed mine.)

5. Eternity is real. There are only two destina-tions—heaven and hell (Mark 16:16). Jesus came to give you a home in heaven (John 14:3).

This can only take place by a sweeping yieldedness, per-sonally and corporately, to Romans 8:11:

> But if the Spirit of Him who raised Jesus from the dead lives in you, He who raised Christ from the

dead will also give life to your mortal bodies through
His Spirit that lives in you.

Notice the contingency. Also take note that this infilling of the Holy Spirit is for mortal, not immortal, bodies. This power is for our lives on earth, not in heaven.

The people of God assigned to this desperate hour are a revolutionary, revenant remnant of revivalists destined to restore a nation, revitalize a civilization, and rescue a generation!

I sense the moisture of miracles in the air. It's raining upstream. There's a downpour coming—a culture-shaking, God-exalting, devil-defeating revival of Pentecostal power if—only if! I am witnessing the resurrection of Holy Ghost believers and Holy Ghost churches rising up from the boiling cauldron of ecumenicalism where everyone is a preacher and everything is a church. We are setting ourselves on a categorical collision course with the forces of darkness! We're taking our families, our churches, and our cities back. We are freeing ourselves from the restraints of religion and ritual, denominationalism and demon power, from terror and timidity—and tomorrow, we change the world! Pentecostal revival if—only if!

CONCLUSION

Last words are of vital importance and are of the most profound significance when uttered by the Lord Jesus Christ. It had been 40 short, yet creatively orchestrated days by His Father since the power of sin, satan, and death had been broken like fetters from the neck of the human family on Calvary's angry beam. It was finished, but by no means was it over. God never creates a consummation without His next initiation in place. There had been a rattling at the gates of damnation. The crucified Prince of Heaven had lifted them from their primeval hinges and flung them into the darkened abyss. It was the morning of the third day after the singular event upon which everything forever changed.

The resurrection is the unanswerable demonstration of the profoundest fact concerning Jesus of Nazareth, "He is not here. For He has risen, as He said" (Matthew 28:6). This is the crown jewel of our faith, the harbinger of our hope. Every prophetic utterance having thus been fulfilled, the Lord Jesus appeared to the first herald of the New Covenant, Mary of Magdala, out of whom He had cast seven devils. Near the garden tomb, the Lord comforted her and directed her to share the news of His resurrection with His disciples. King Jesus then appeared to two followers making the seven-mile, three-hour walk from Jerusalem to Emmaus, and revealing Himself to them in the breaking of bread. Our Lord met personally with Simon Peter, reaffirming their relationship despite Peter's thrice denial of Him. Then in a dark room where the disciples were hiding for fear their lives were now at risk, Jesus suddenly stood among them. At that moment the greatest understatement ever recorded was made. If ever there had been an incident when the inspired writer of the biblical text would have been tempted to exaggerate, it would most certainly have been here: "And when he had so said, he shewed unto them his hands and his side. Then were the disciples glad, when they saw the Lord" (John 20:20 KJV). They were "glad."

During these eventful 40 days, the risen Savior continued to teach His followers truth regarding the kingdom of God, forgiveness, and, of course, the Holy Spirit. In fact, He announced the Holy Spirit would anoint them to be His witnesses who were to spread His glorious gospel to all nations (Acts 1:8).

At the close of those five weeks and five days, the time had come for Calvary's conquering King to release His concluding commission to His disciples, as well as to you and me. Here are those final words encapsulated in Mark 16:15-16, "Go into all the world and preach the gospel to every creature. He who believes and is baptized will be saved. But he who does not believe will be condemned." Verse 20 continues, "Then they went forth and preached everywhere, the Lord working with them and confirming the word through the accompanying signs. Amen."

ENDNOTES

1 Ashton Parsley, Mark Arthur II, "Holy Spirit Come," Harvest Music Live, *Light the World on Fire* (2015).

2 Rod Parsley, *God's End-Time Calendar: The Prophetic Meaning Behind Celestial Events and Seasons* (Lake Mary, FL: Charisma House, 2015), 90-91.

3 Ibid., 91.

4 Ibid., 92-93.

5 M.J. Cartwright, "The Old Ship of Zion," music by Daniel B. Towner (cir. 1889).

6 Justin Martyr, *Dialogue with Trypho*, Chapter LXXXII, https://www.ccel.org/ccel/schaff/anf01.viii.iv.lxxxii.html.

7 Irenaeus, *Against Heresies*, Book II, chapter 32, sections 4-5; https://www.newadvent.org/fathers/0103232.htm.

8 John Chrysostom, Talbot W. Chambers, trans., Homily 29 on First Corinthians, http://www.newadvent.org/fathers/220129.htm.

9 Rod Parsley, *The Miracles of Jesus* (Columbus, OH: Results Publishing, 2019), 10-12.

10 Ibid., 12-16.

11 "Global Pentecostalism," https://www.gordonconwell.edu/center-for-global-christianity/research/global-pentecostalism.

12 Jannik Lindner, "Evangelism Statistics," Worldmetrics Report 2024, June 18, 2024, https://worldmetrics.org/evangelism-statistics.

13   Michael Parrott, "Street Level Evangelism, Where is the Space for the Local Evangelist," in *Acts Evangelism* (Spokane, WA, 1993), 9-11.

14   R. J. Krejcir Ph.D., "Statistics and Reasons for Church Decline," Francis A. Schaeffer Institute of Church Leadership Development, at Church Leadership (2007), http://www.churchleadership.org/apps/articles/default.asp?articleid=42346.

15   Rod Parsley, *Idolatry in America* (Lake Mary, FL: Charisma House, 2024), 158.

16   Rod Parsley, *50 Moments of Pentecostal History* (Columbus, OH: Results Publishing, 2022), 87-88.

17   Ibid., 62-63.

18   Donnie McDonald, "Filling the Spiritual Vacuum," ONE Magazine, October/November 2023 (Antioch, TN), https://www.nafwb.org/onemag/octnov2023.htm.

19   Andreas Moser, "Coca Cola is everywhere," April 2, 2017, https://andreasmoser.blog/2017/04/02/coca-cola.

20   Lincoln's Lyceum Address was delivered to the Young Men's Lyceum of Springfield, Illinois.

21   Charles Haddon Spurgeon, "The Soul-Winner," in Metropolitan Tabernacle Pulpit Volume 22, January 20, 1876, https://www.spurgeon.org/resource-library/sermons/the-soul-winner/#flipbook.

22   Rod Parsley, *The Fire Within: A Guide to the Baptism of the Holy Spirit* (Columbus, OH: Results Publishing, 2021), 39-45.

23   Rod Parsley, *Revival If...* (Lake Mary, FL: Charisma House, 2022), 70.

24   Ibid., 71.

25   Quoted in https://www.keylife.org/articles/brennan-manning-on-gods-love.7